HORSE LIFE

True Friend, True Warrior

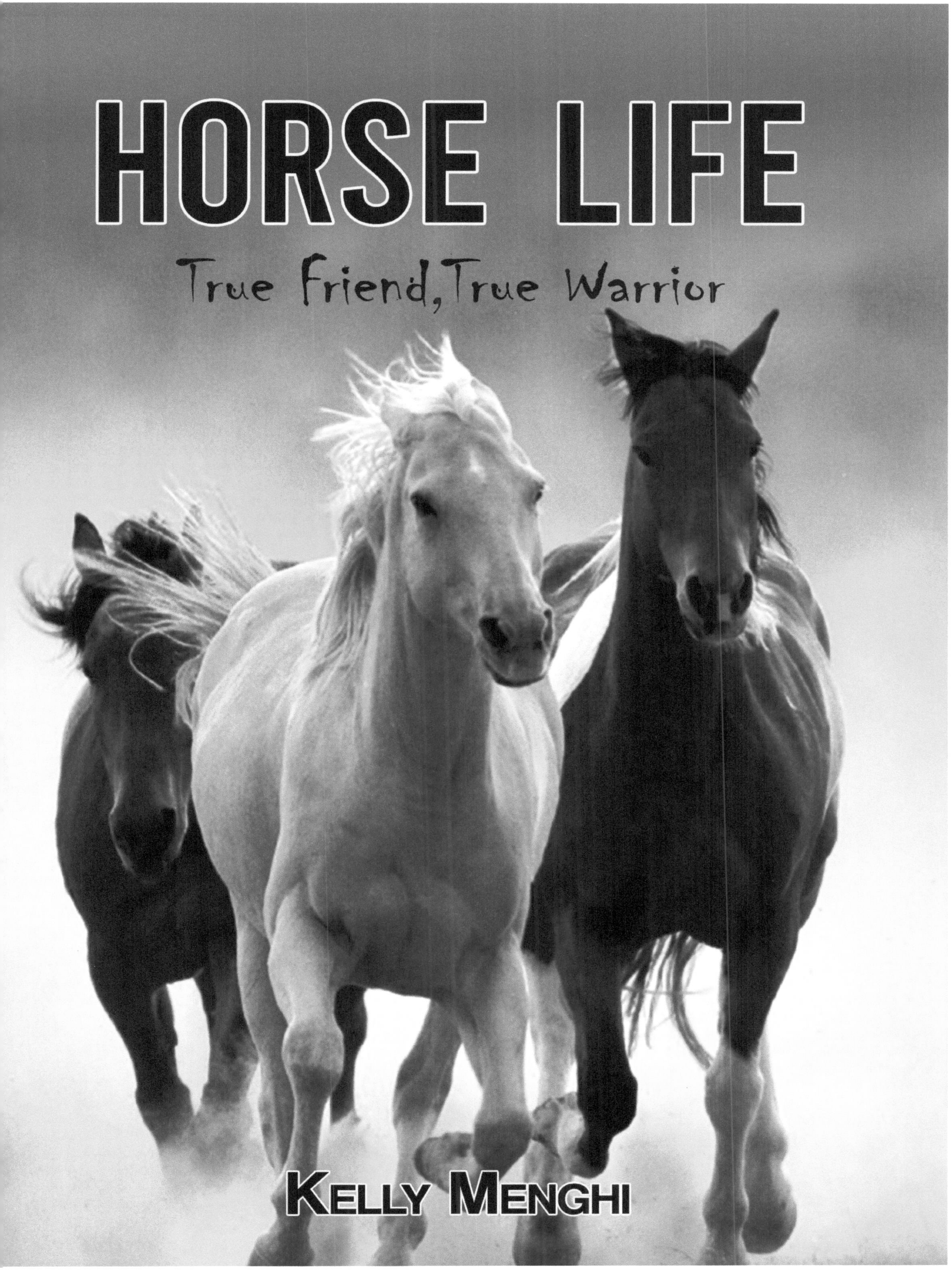

KELLY MENGHI

THE WIND OF HEAVEN IS THAT WHICH BLOWS BETWEEN A HORSE'S EARS.

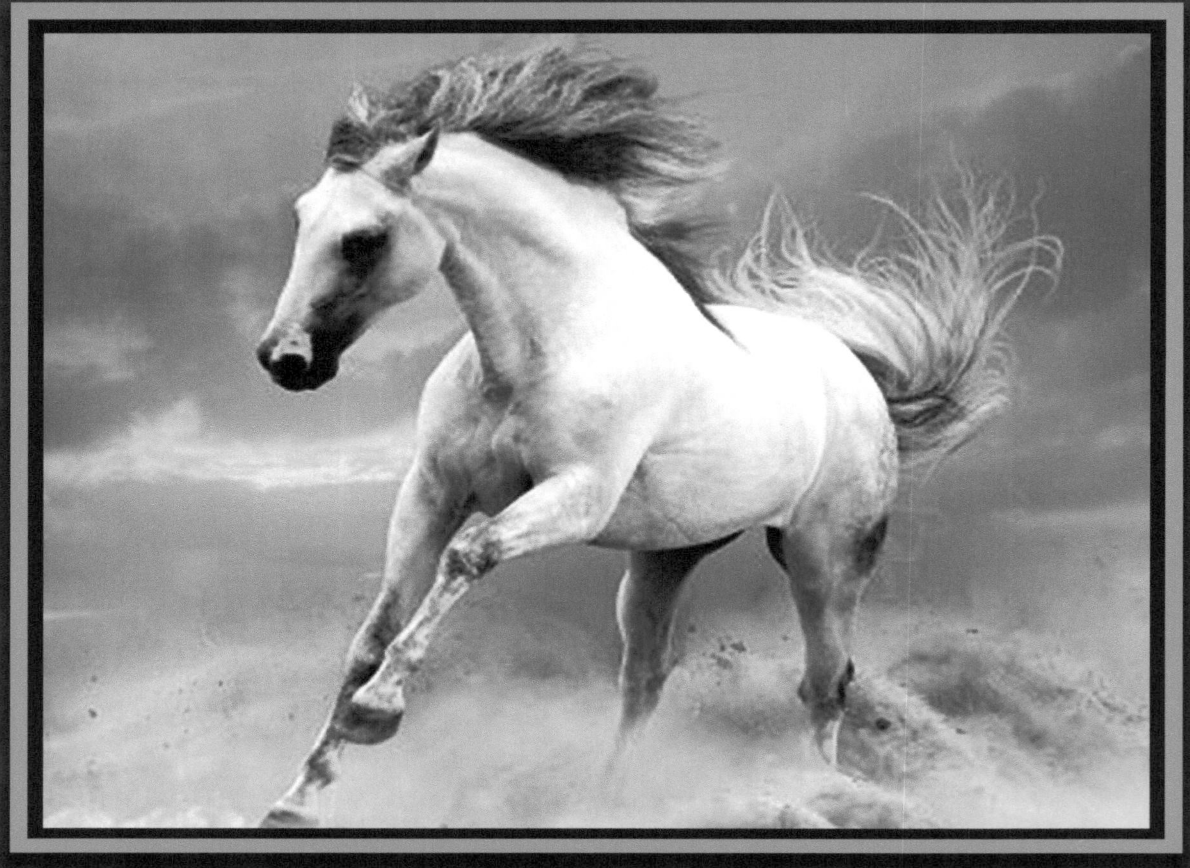

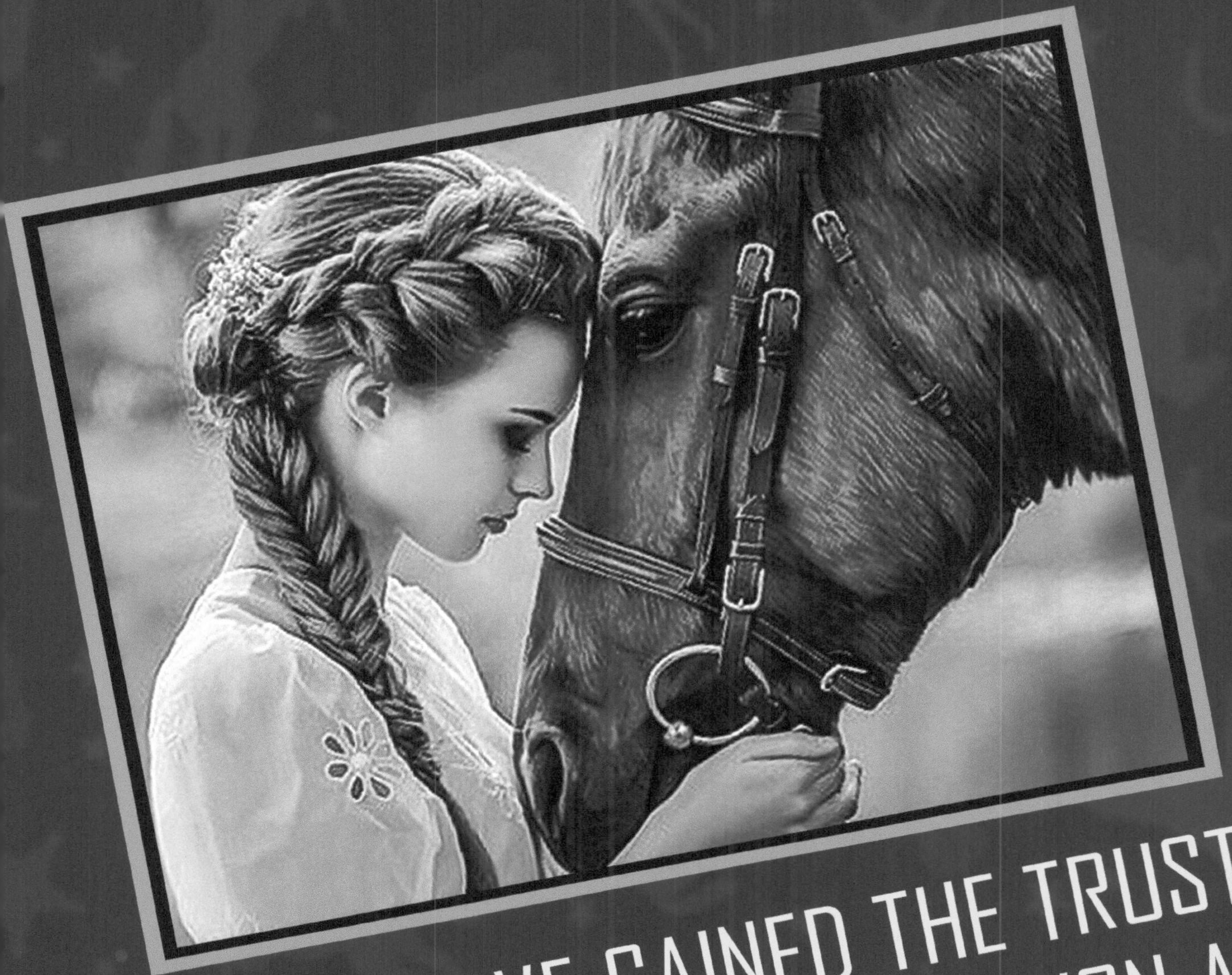

IF YOU HAVE GAINED THE TRUST OF A HORSE, YOU HAVE WON A FRIEND FOR LIFE.

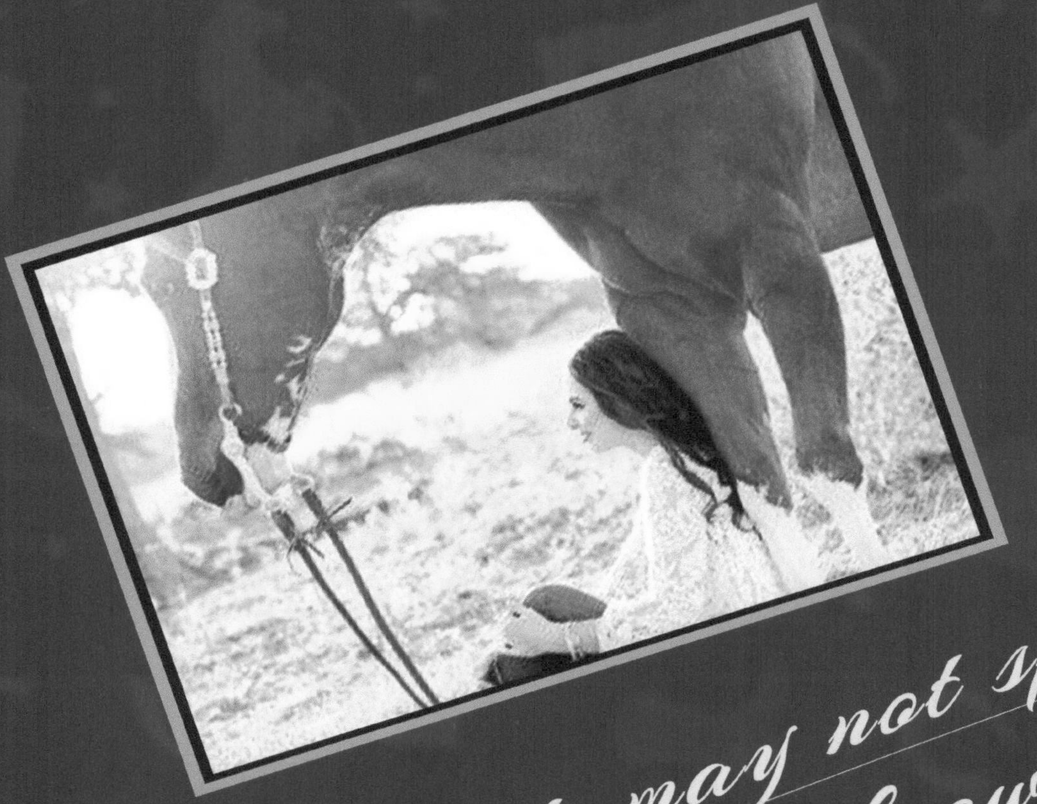

Best friends may not speak,
but at least you know they
are listening!

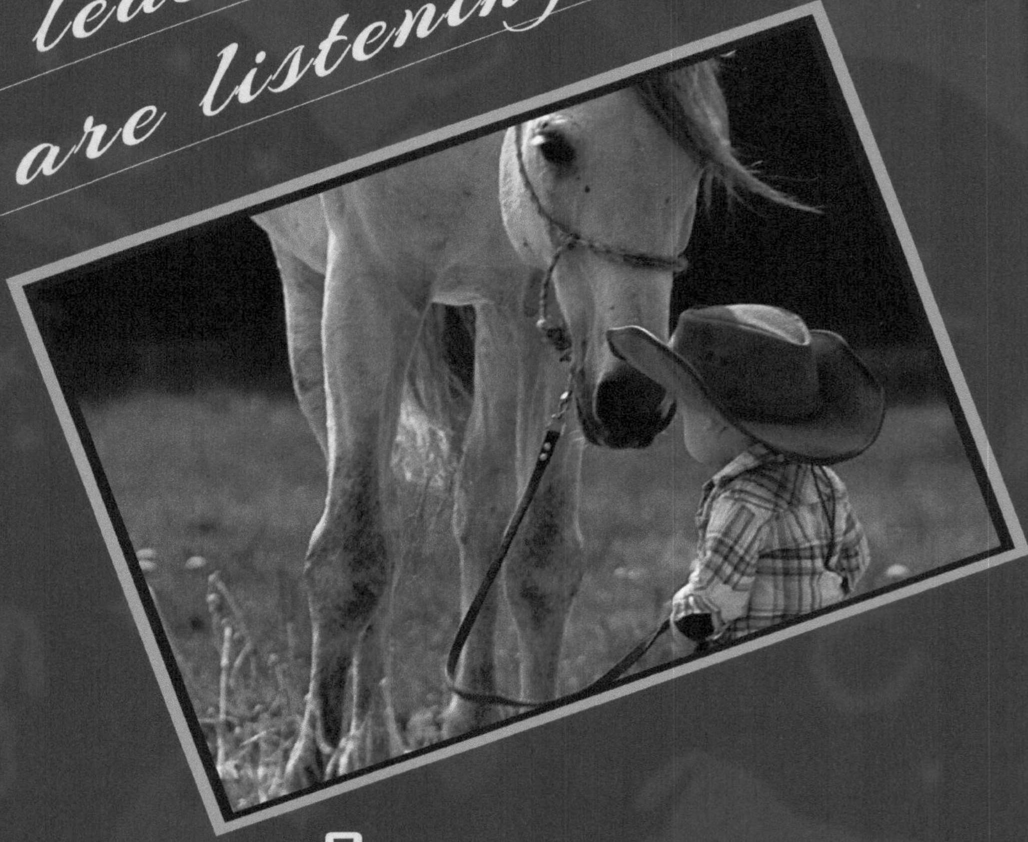

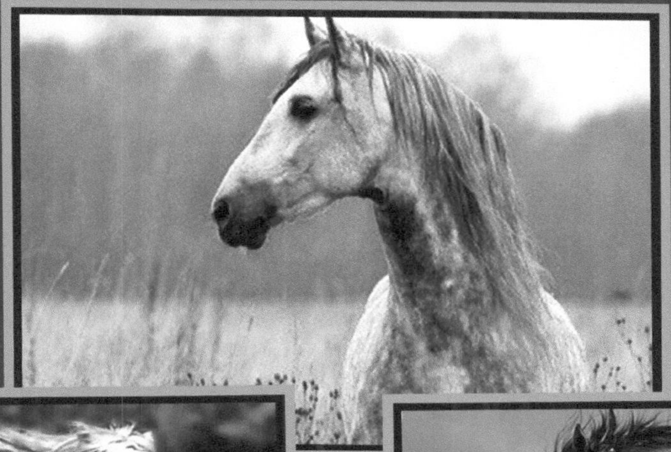

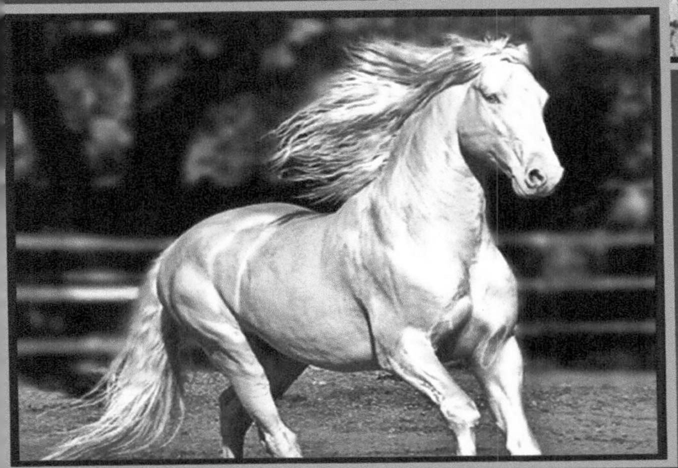

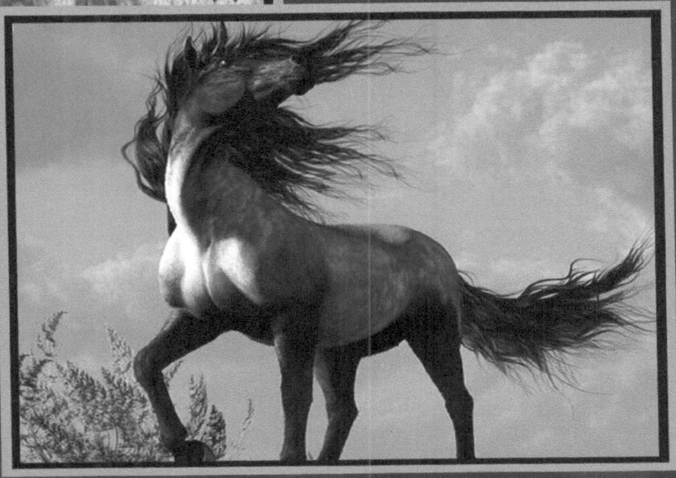

A *HORSE* CAN CHANGE
HE WAY YOU SEE THE
WORLD.

Brave

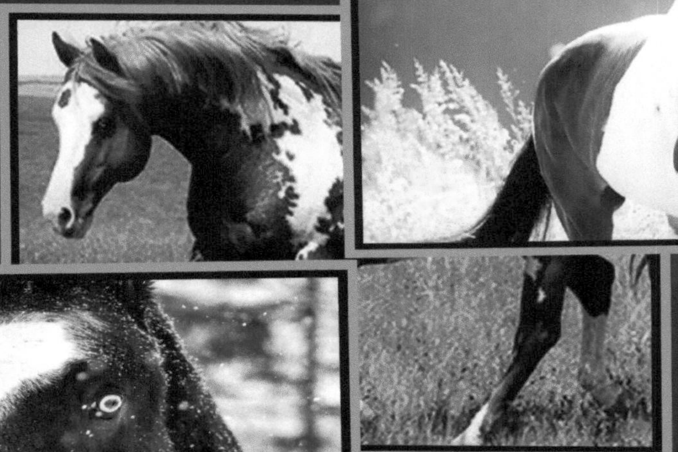

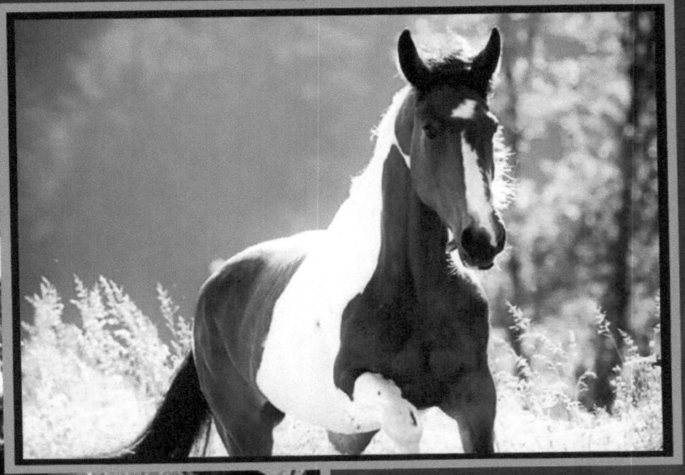

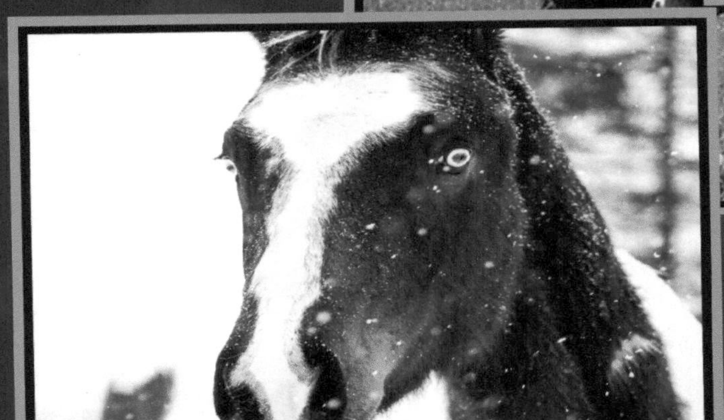

If passion drive you
let reason hold
the reins.

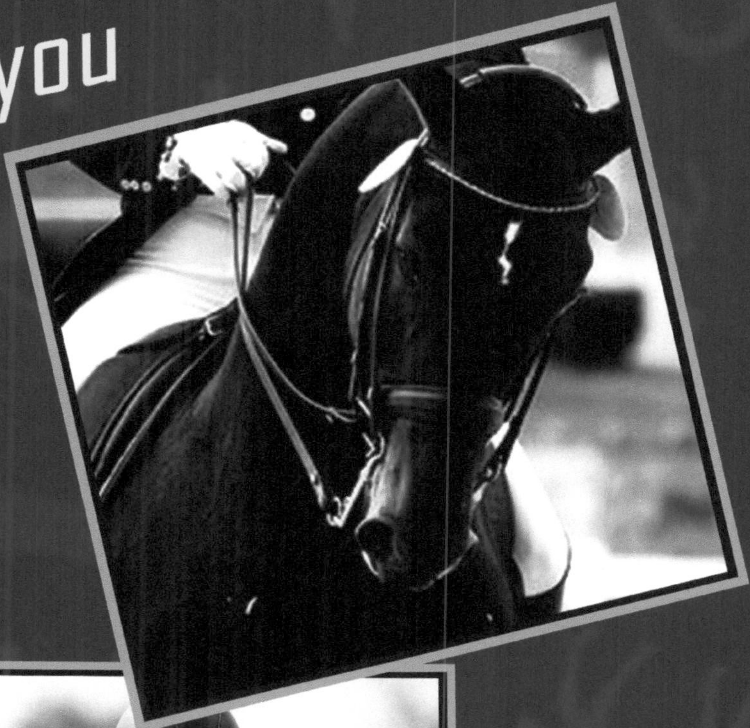

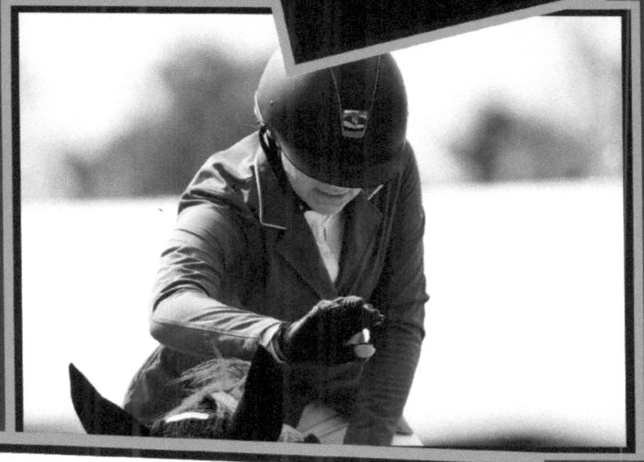

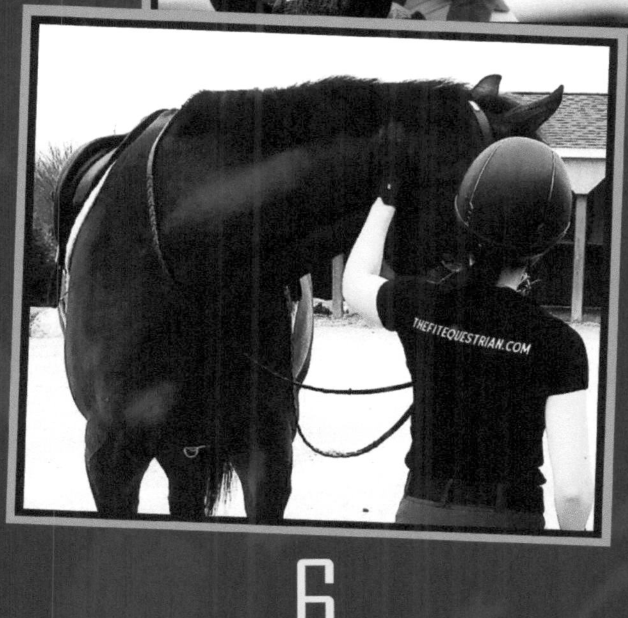

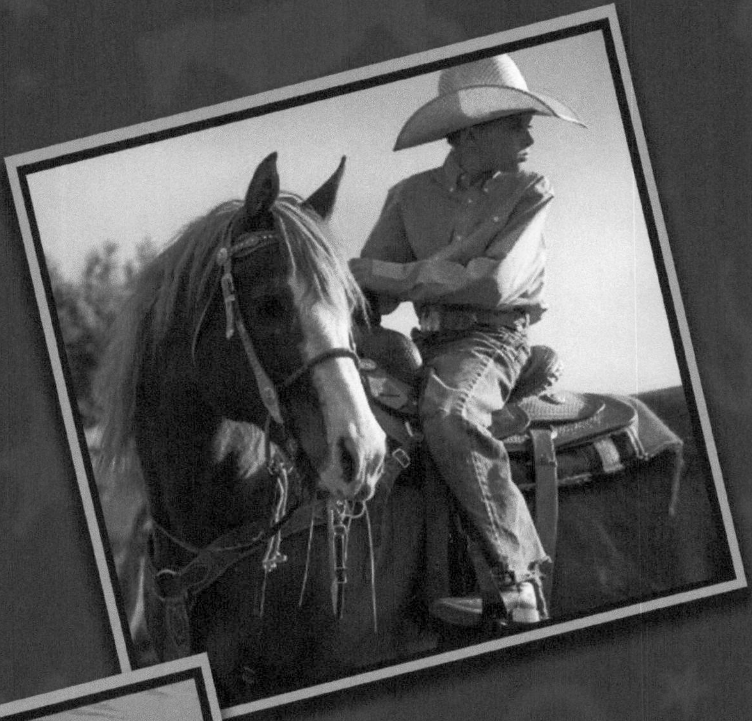

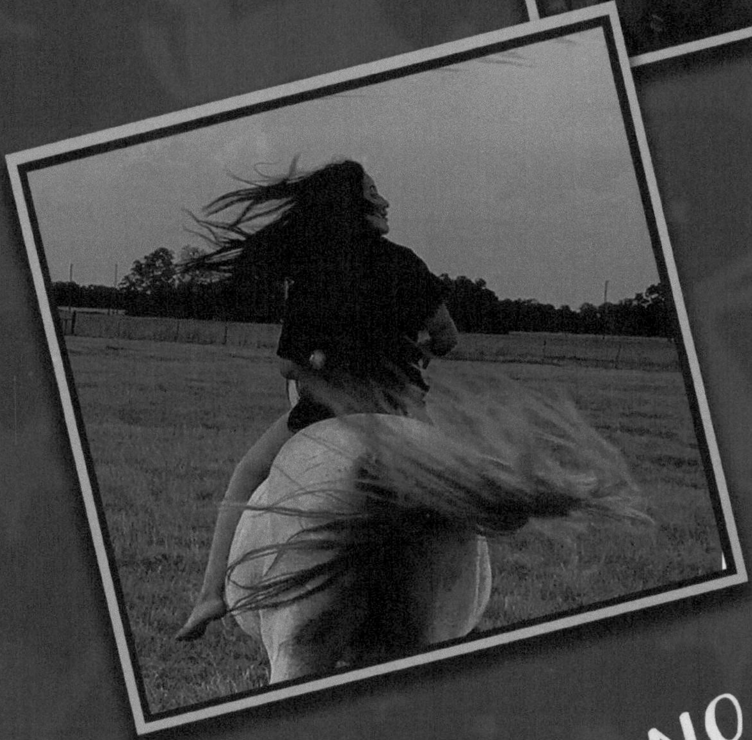

NO HOUR OF LIFE
IS WASTED THAT
IS SPENT IN THE
SADDLE.

To ride a

HORSE

is to

RIDE THE SKY

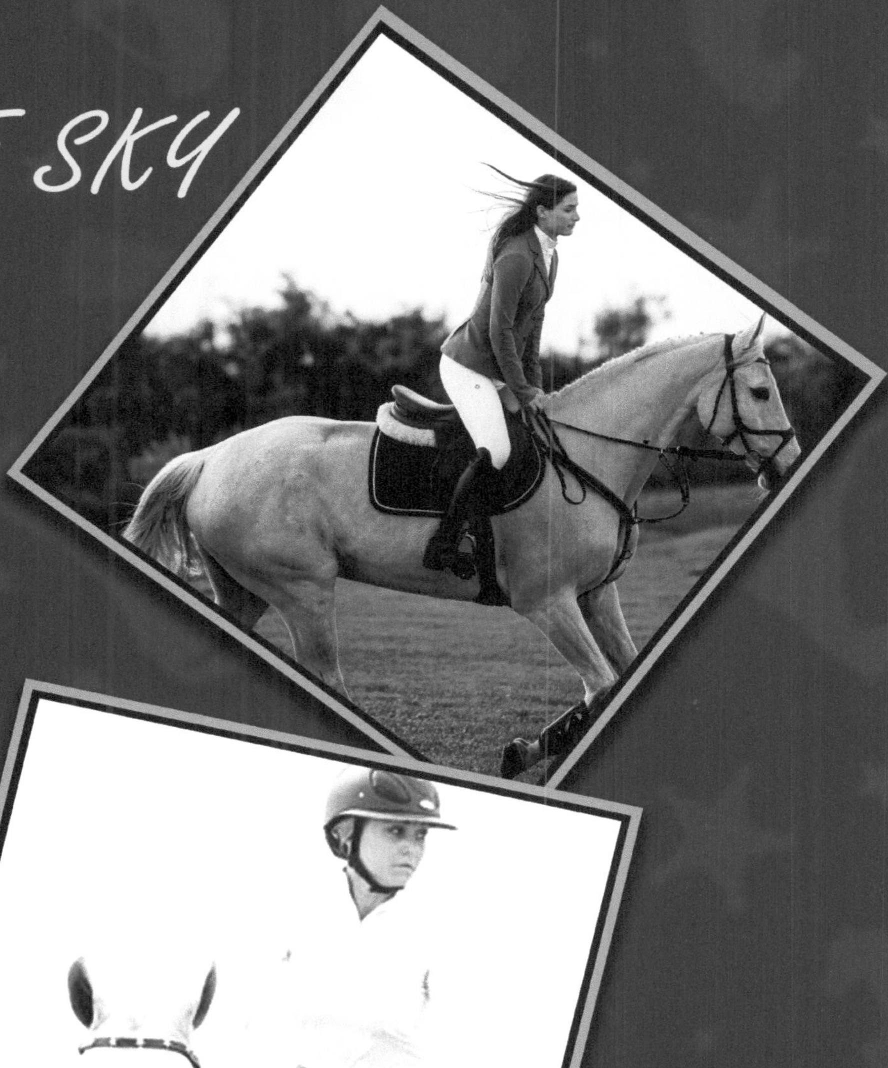

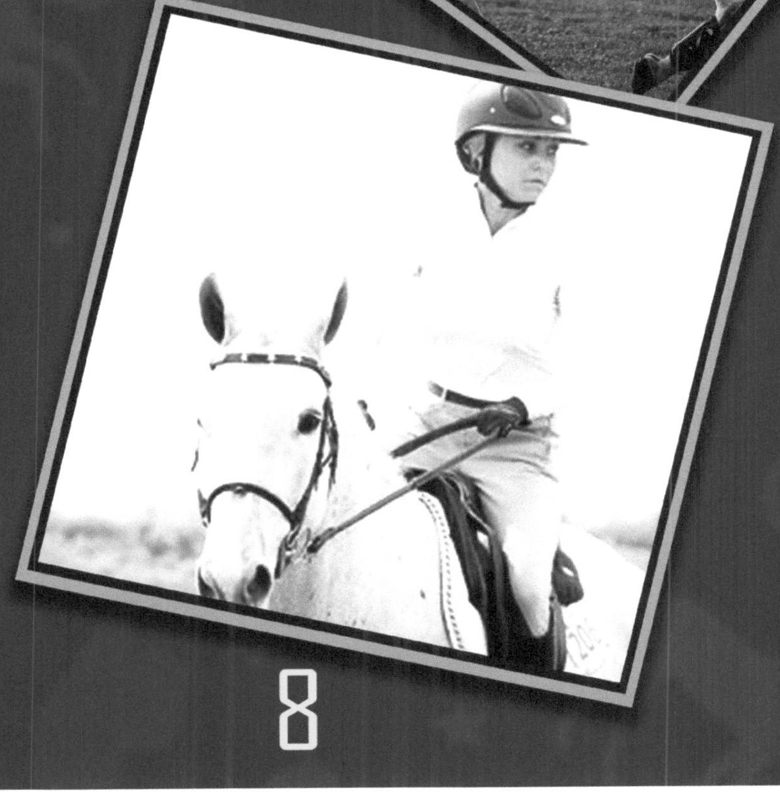

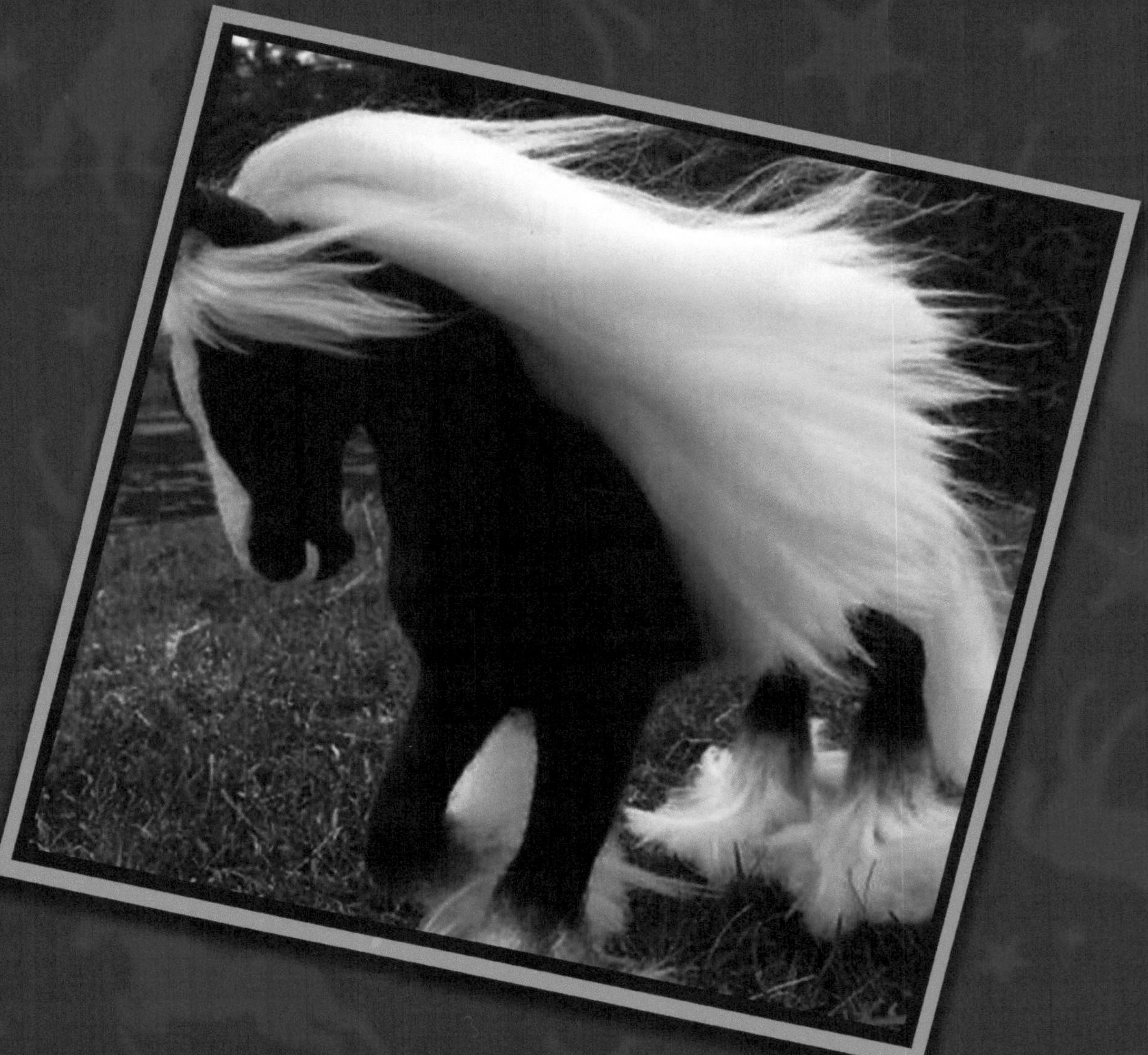

Lovely Horse

F E A R L E S S

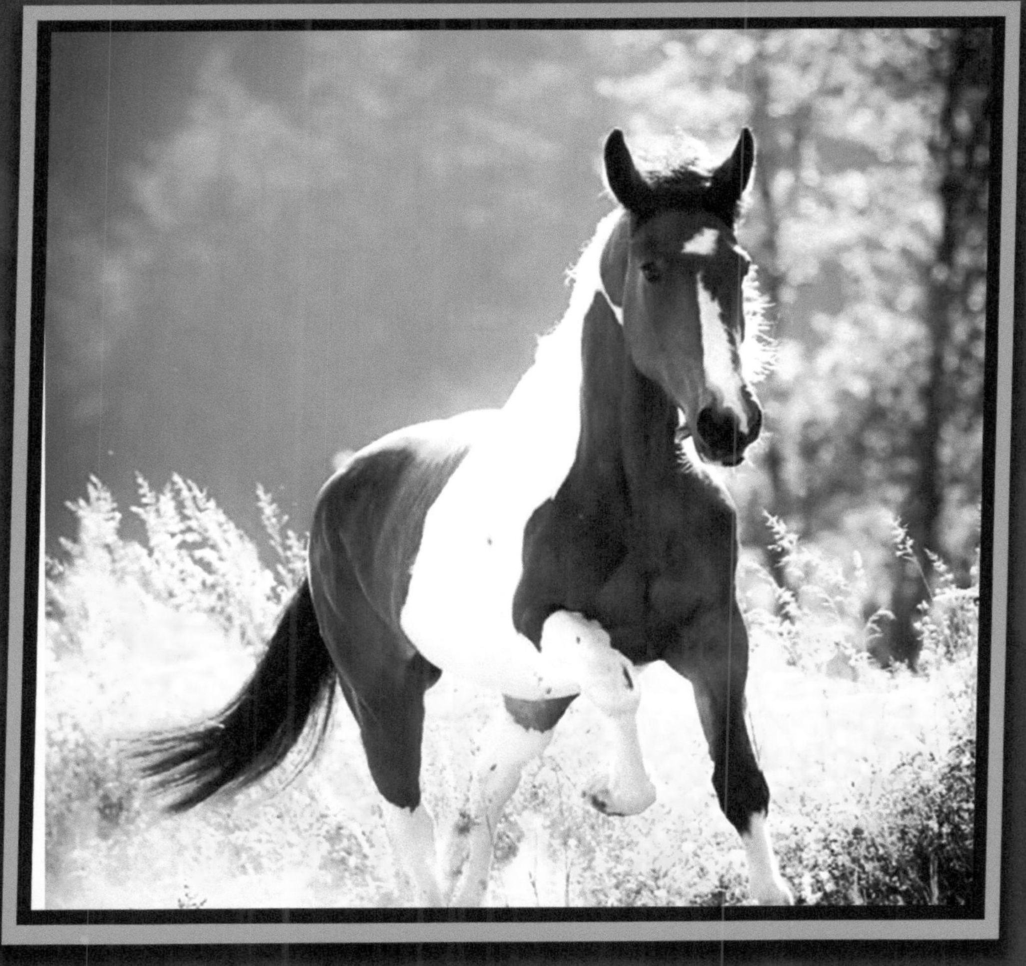

Beautiful Horse

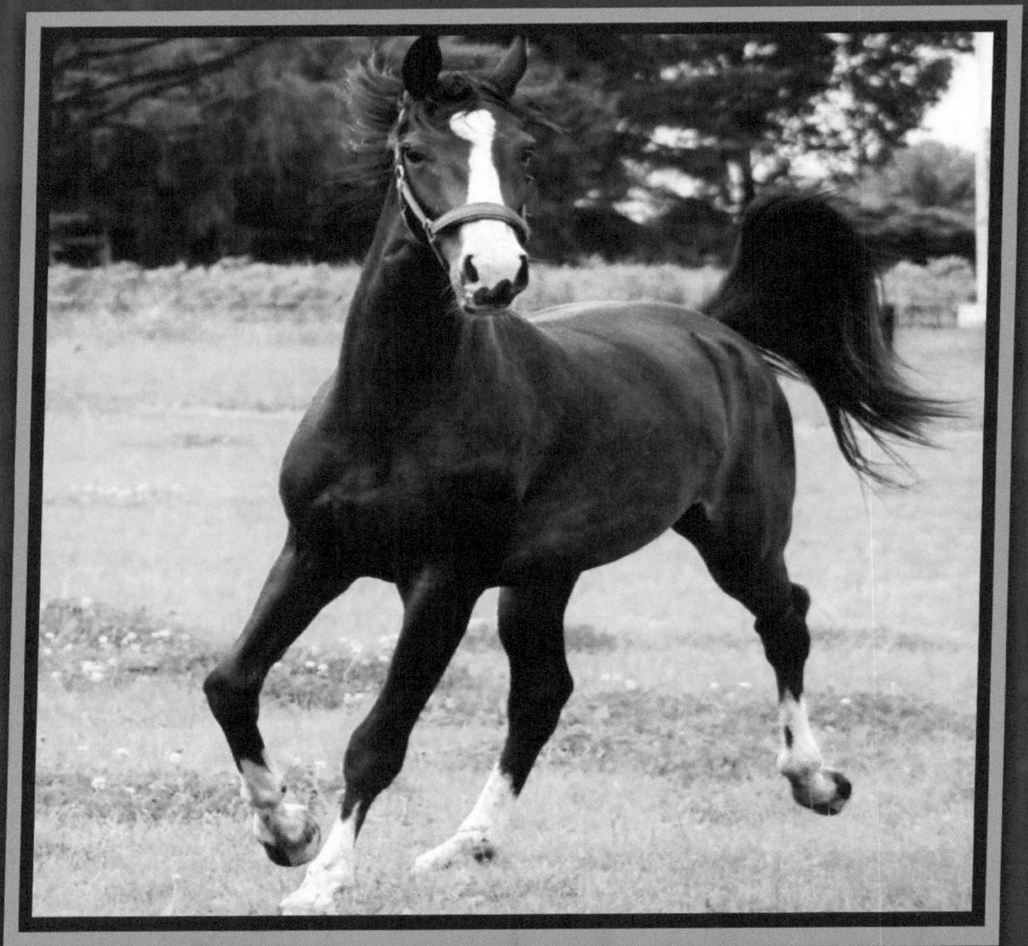

Courage

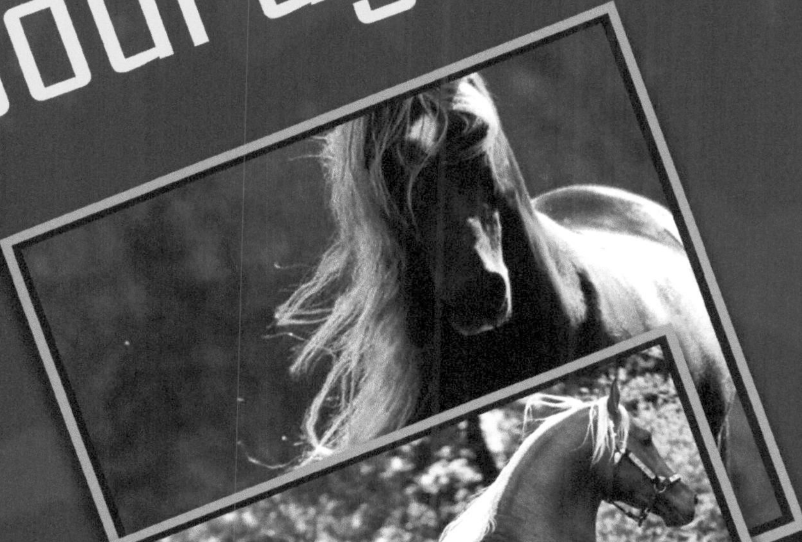

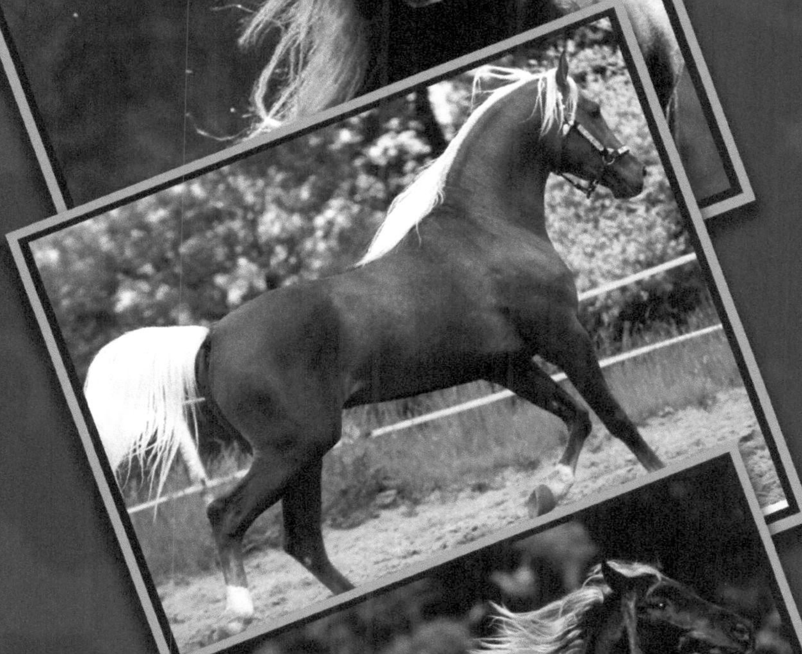

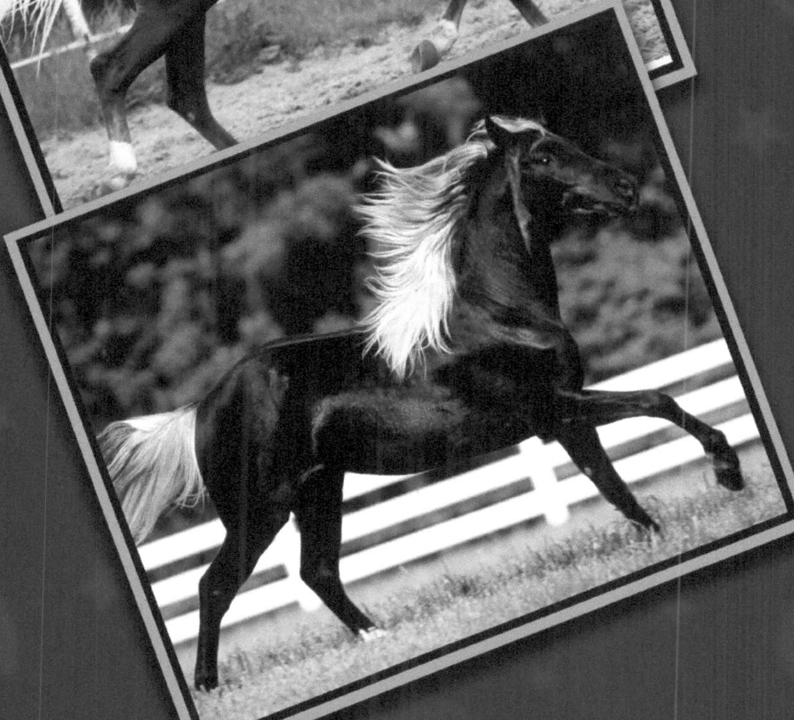

HORSE MAKE YOU HAPPY

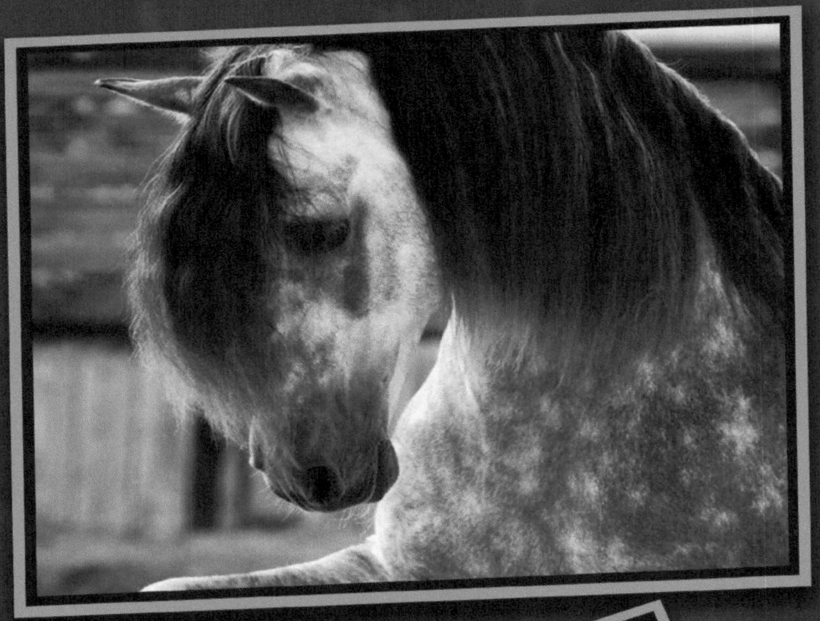

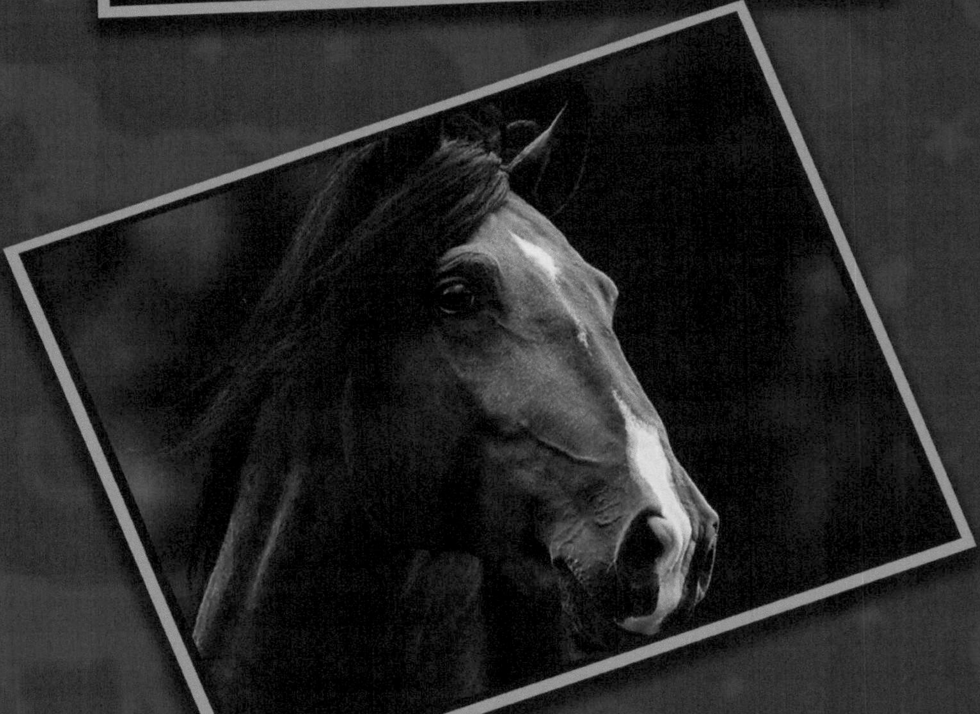

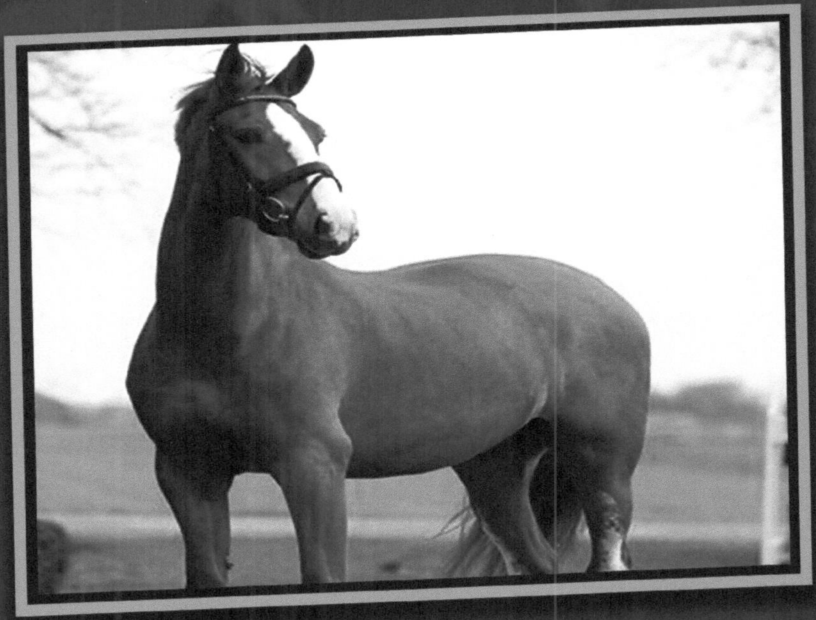

Loving a horse is much easier than loving a person.

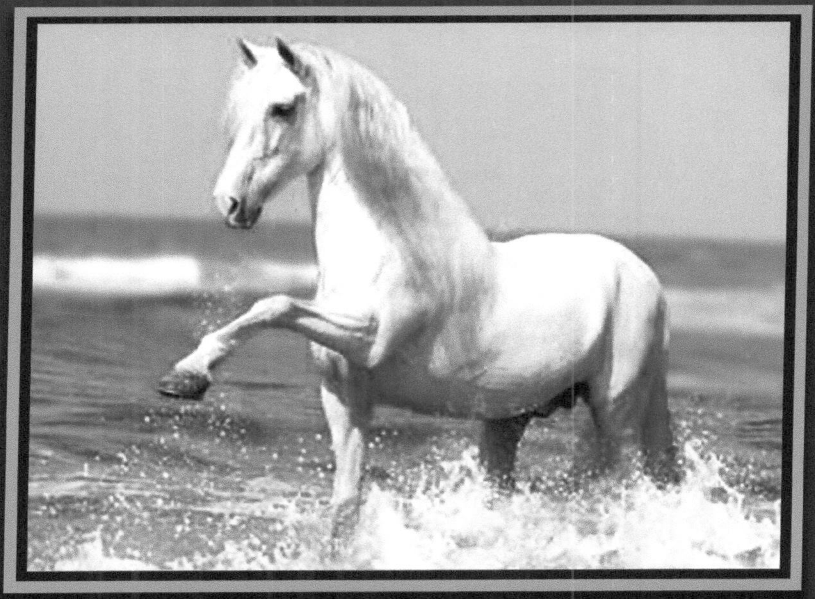

There is no secret between Horse and Rider.

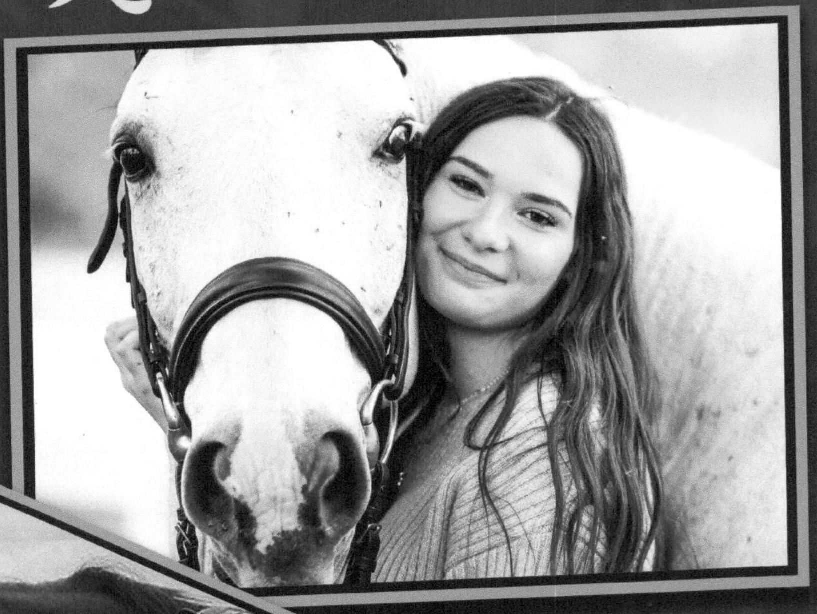

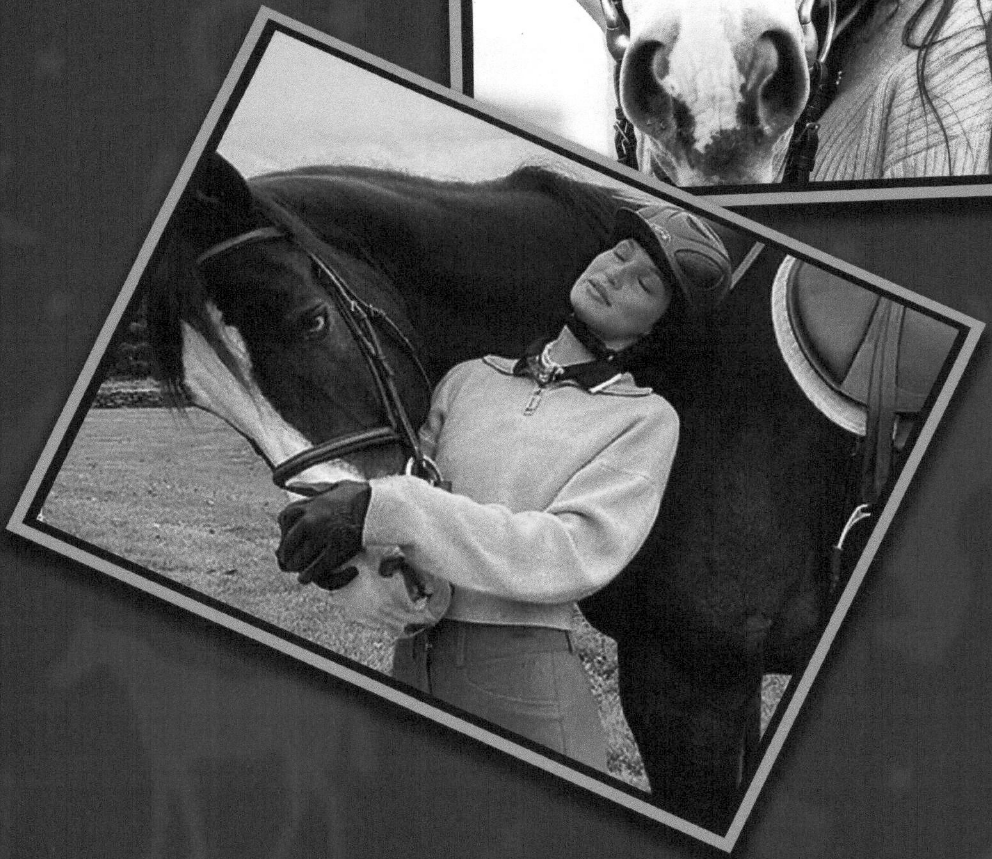

If you want a stable friendship, get a horse.

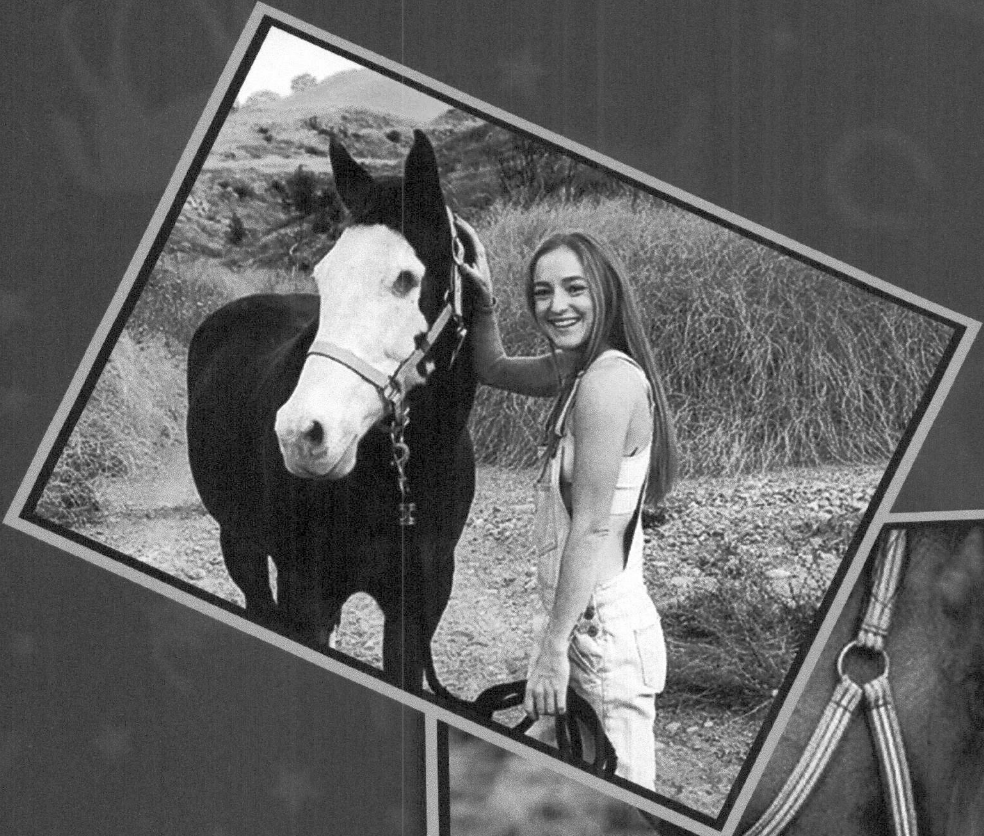

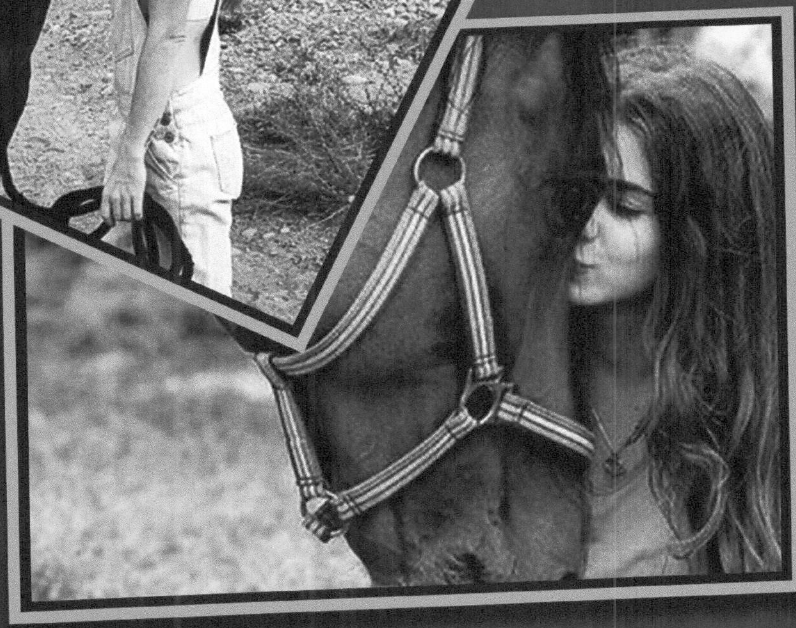

To ride a horse is to fly without wings.

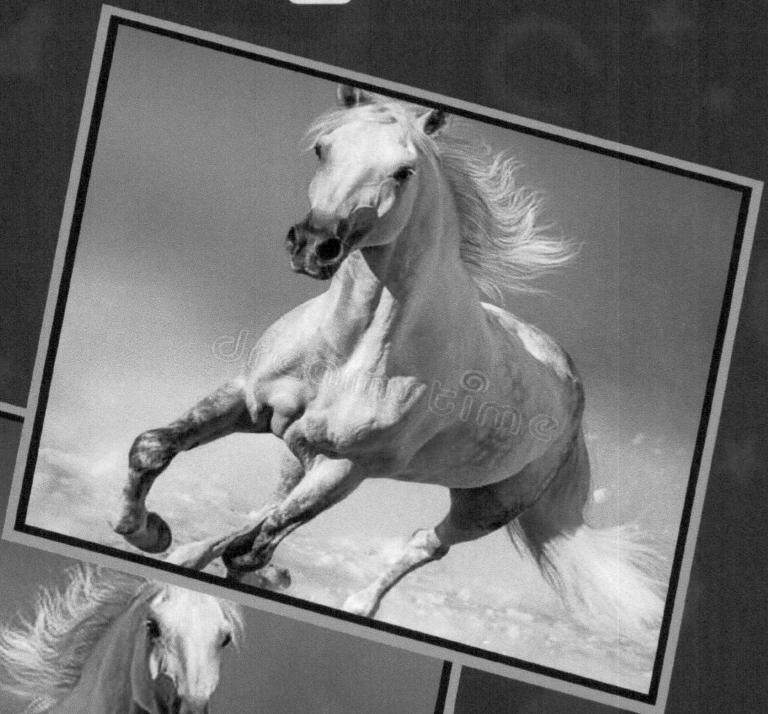

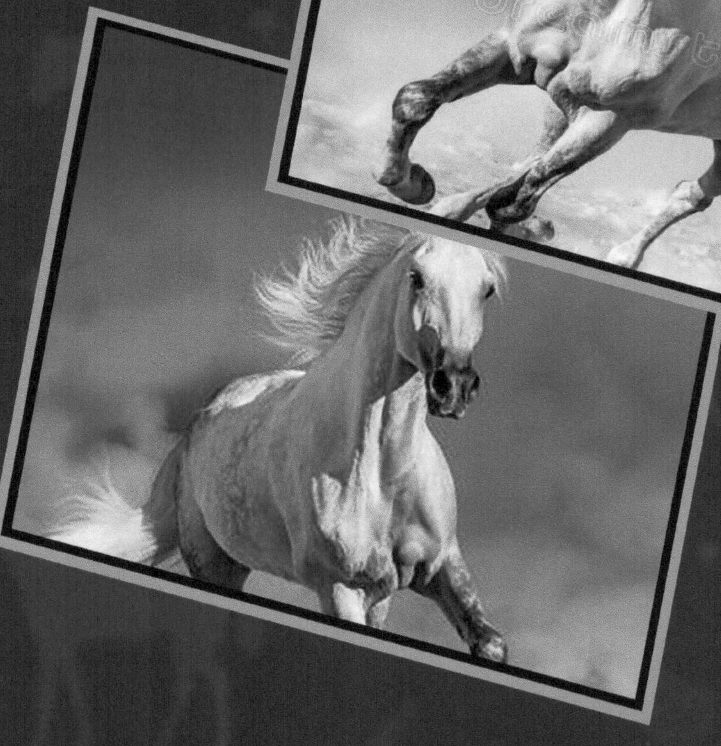

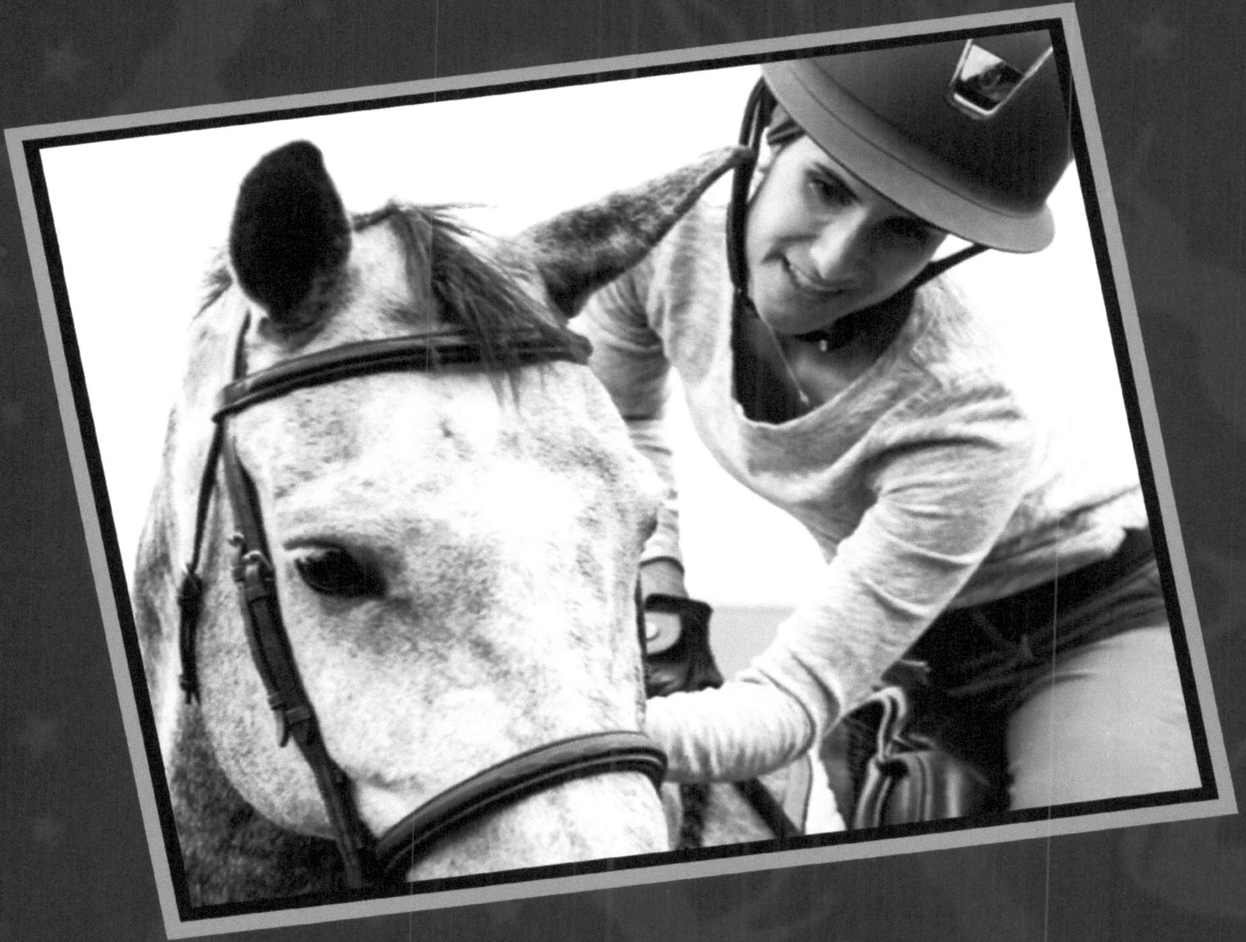

In riding a horse,
we borrow
Freedom

Riding is the best solution of any problems.

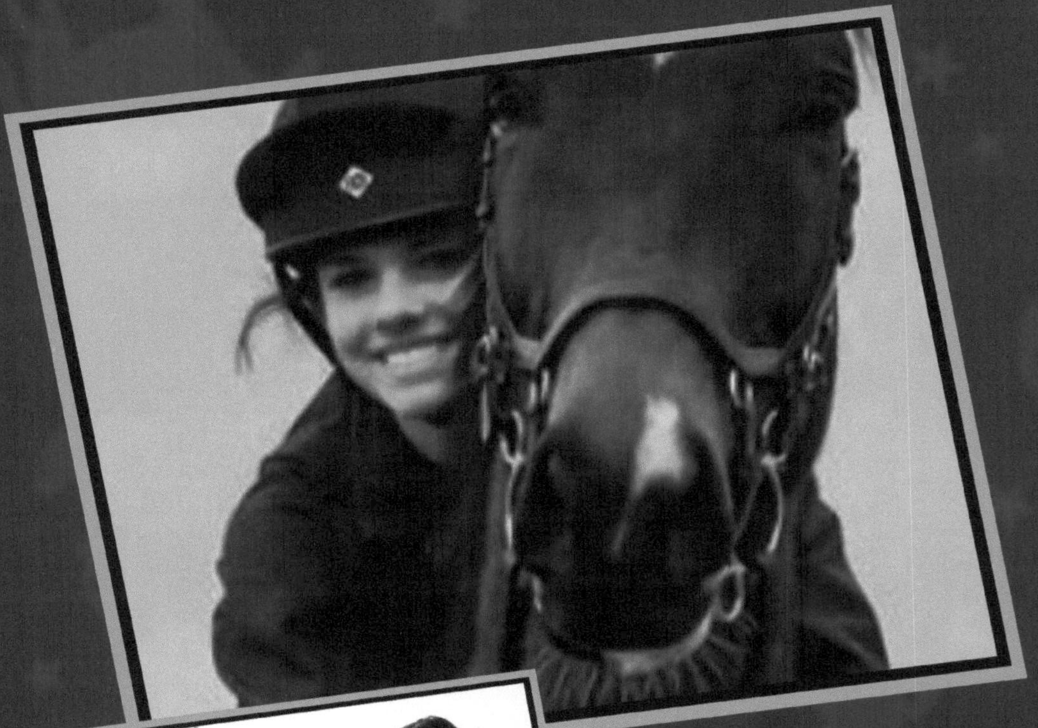

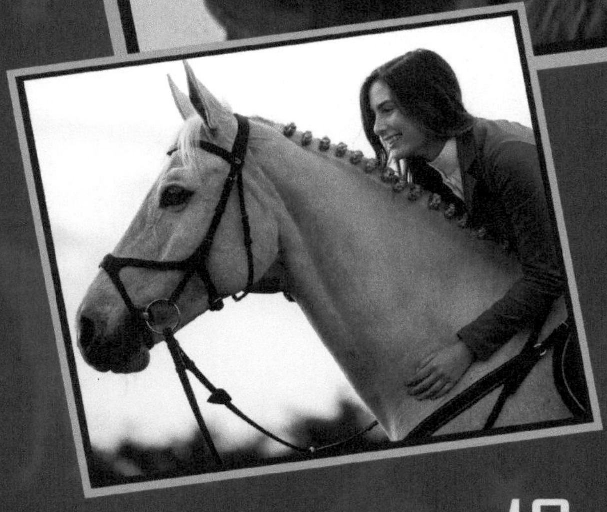

your Horse is
only **Brave**
as you are.

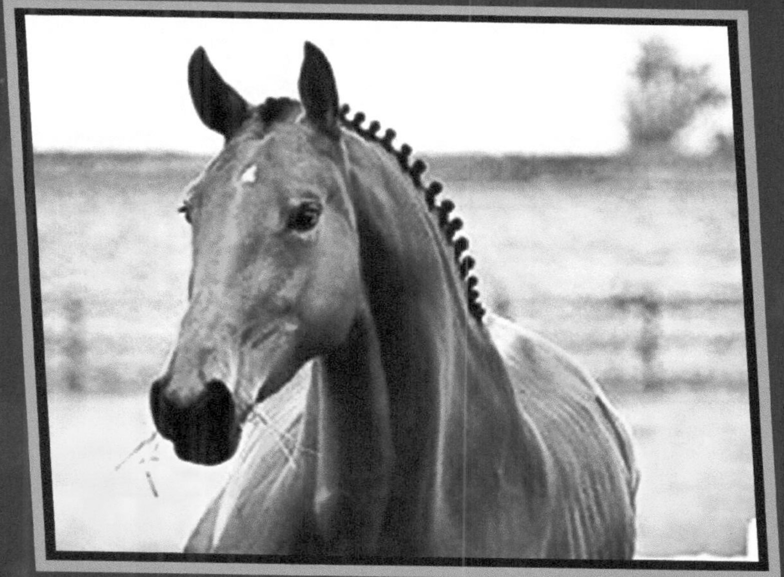

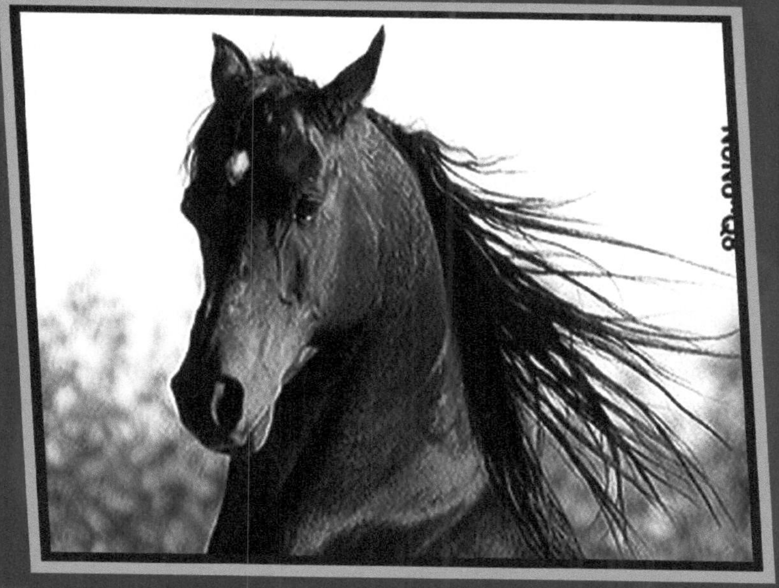

Life without Horse is like taking a breath without Air.

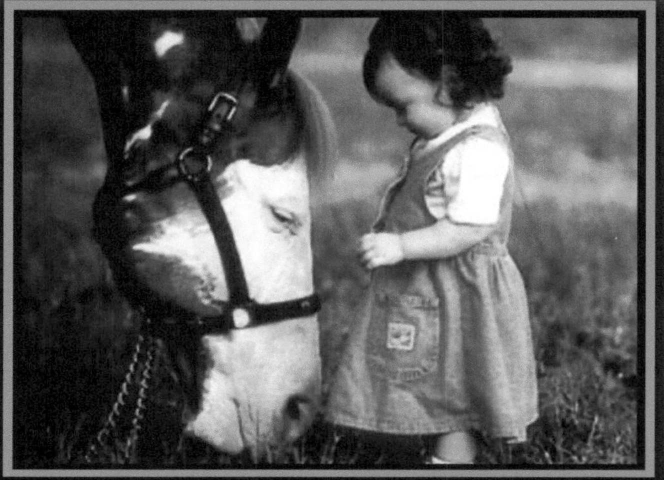

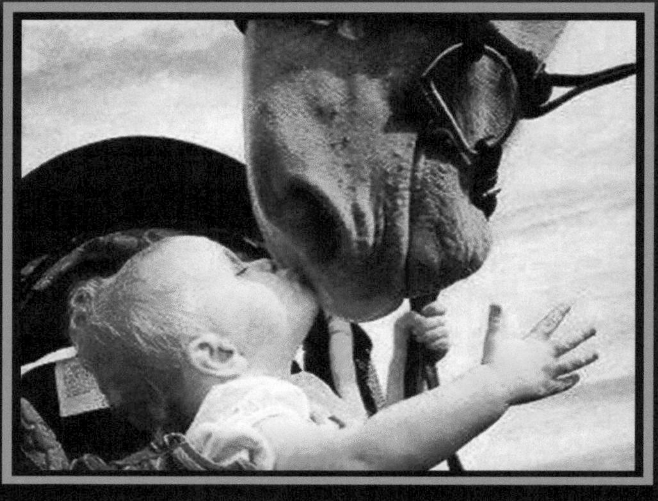

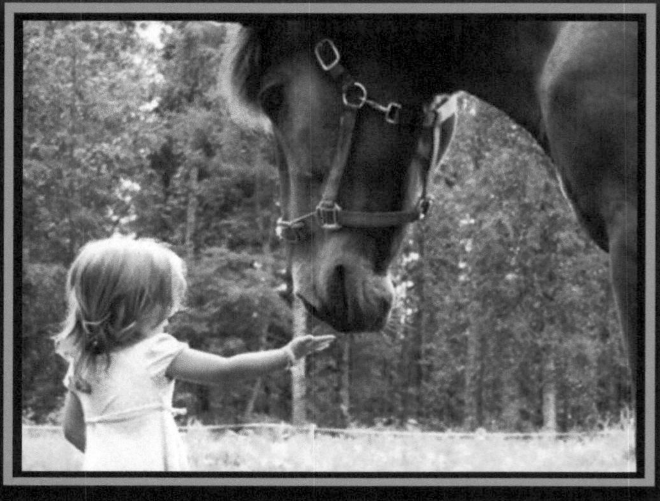

Some best friends never say a word.

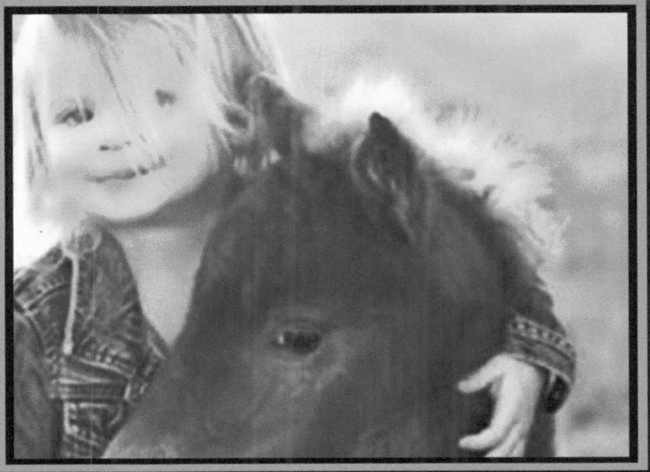

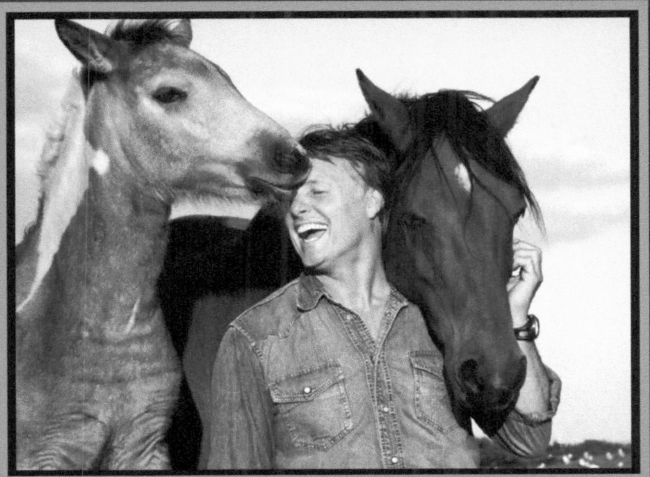

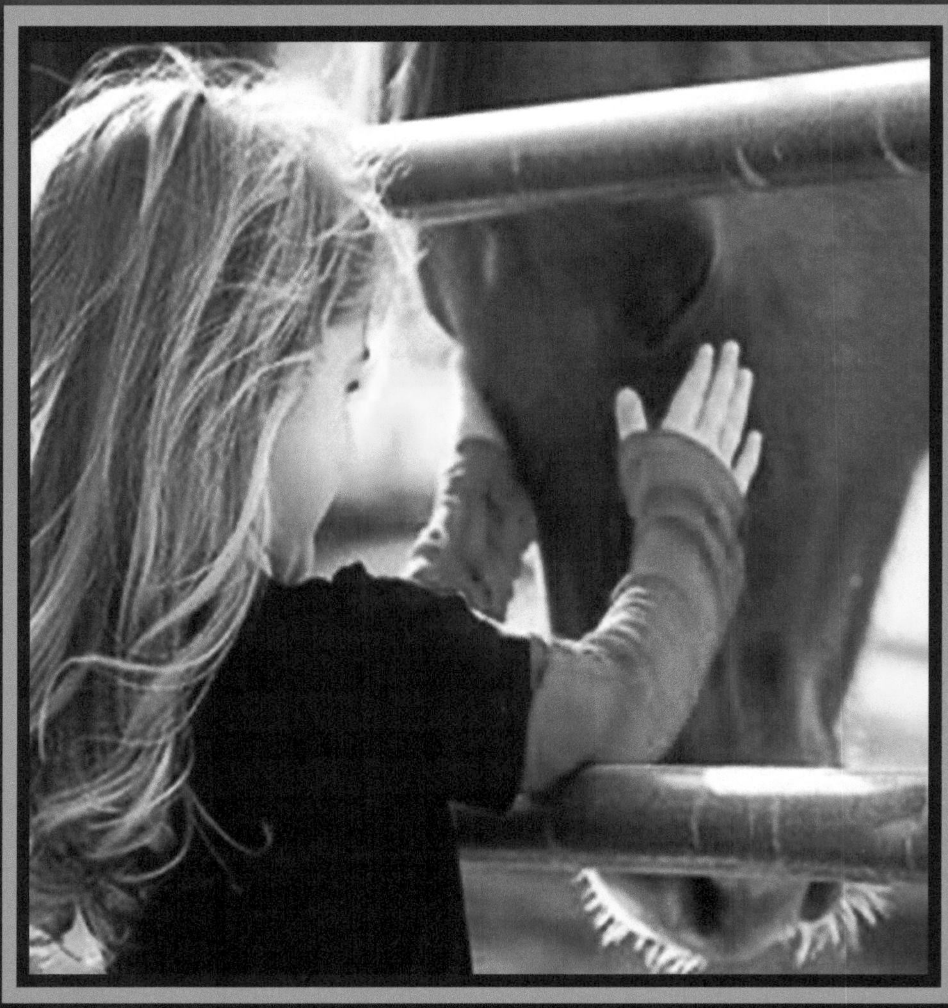

Our perfect companions never
have fewer than four feet.

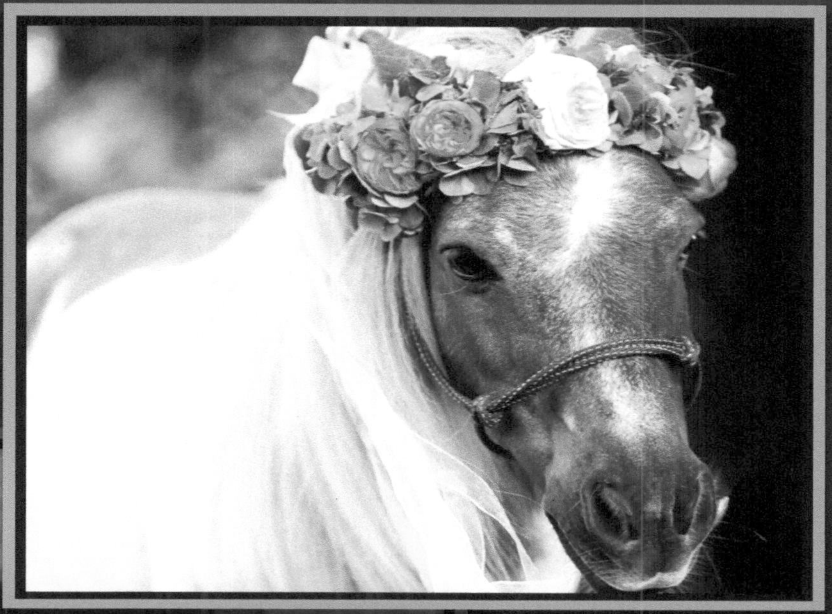

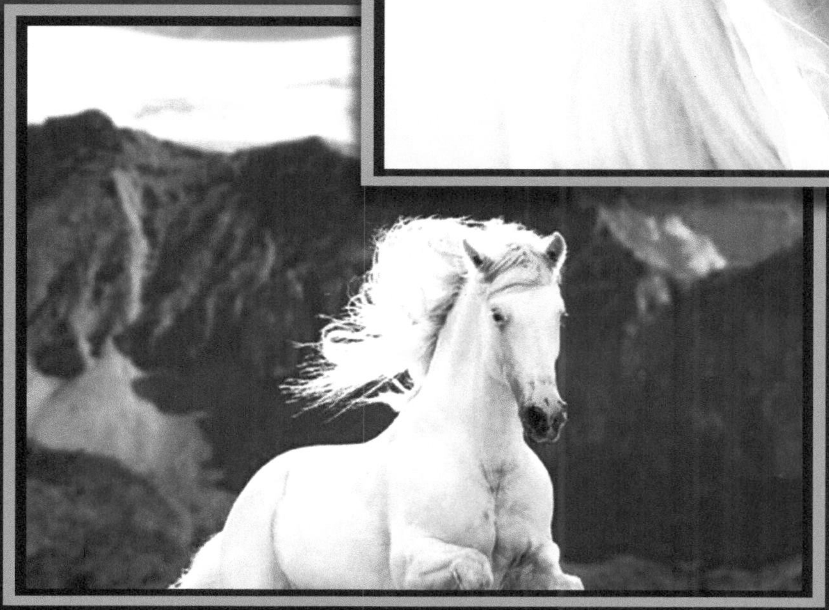

Loving the horse is much easier than loving a person.

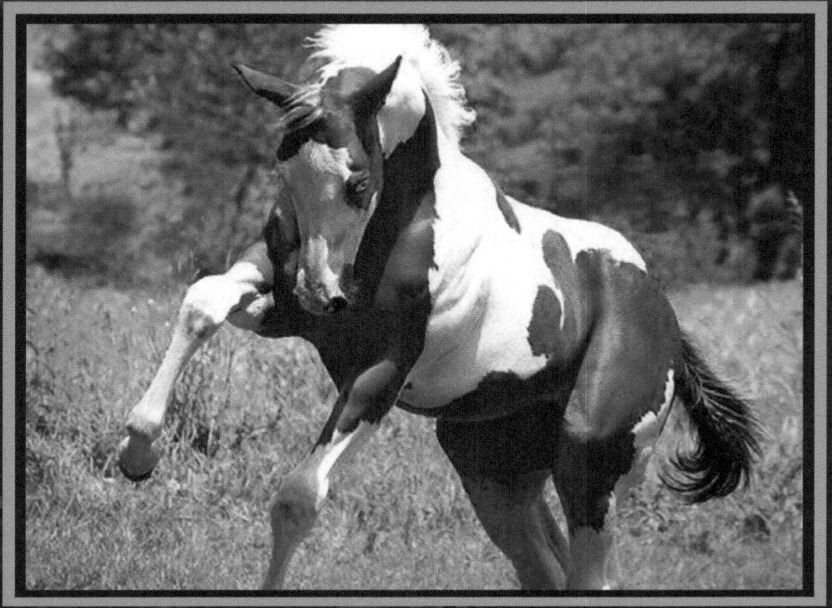

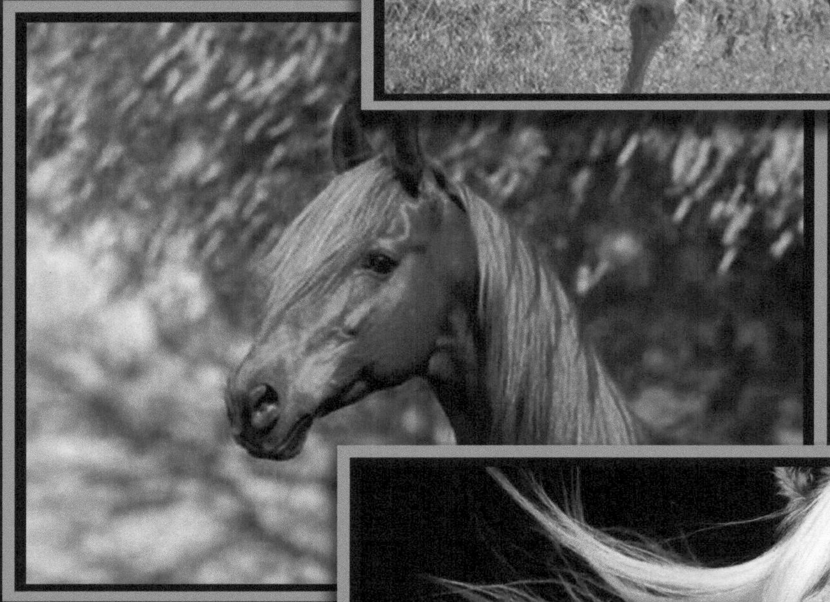

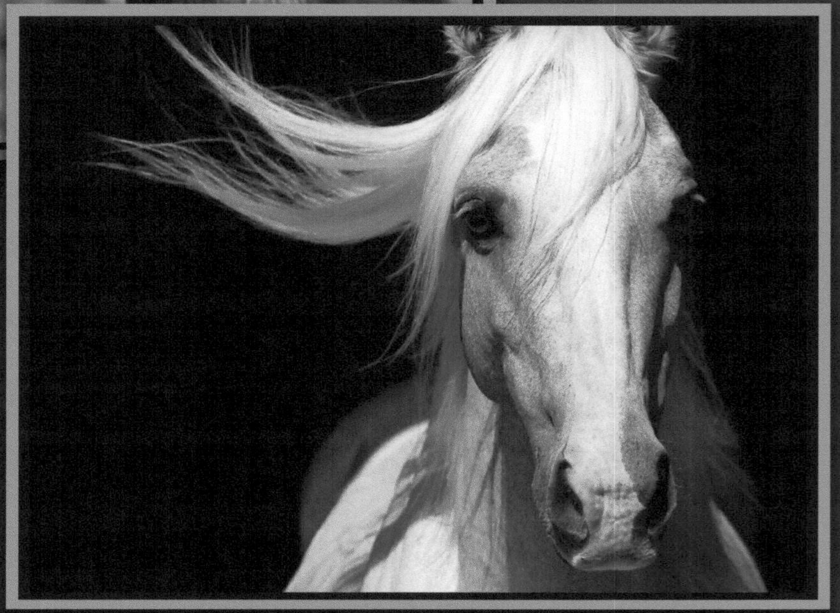

CUTE

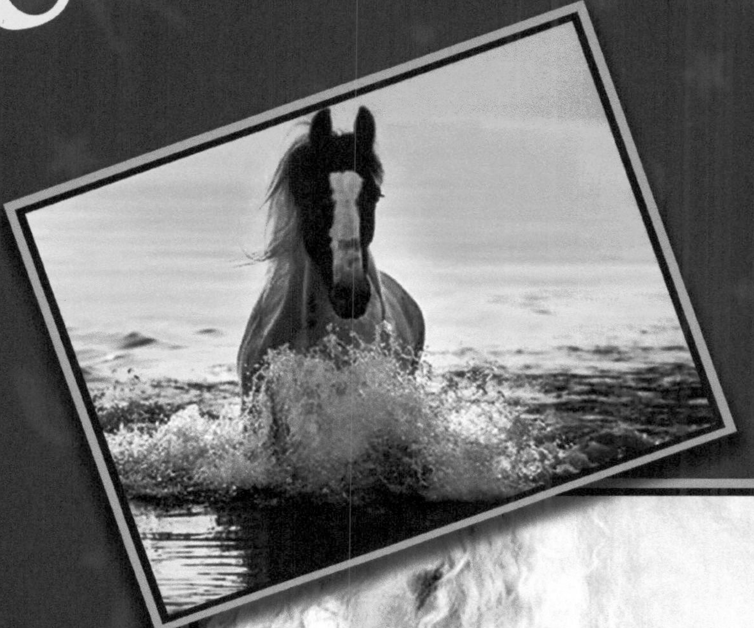

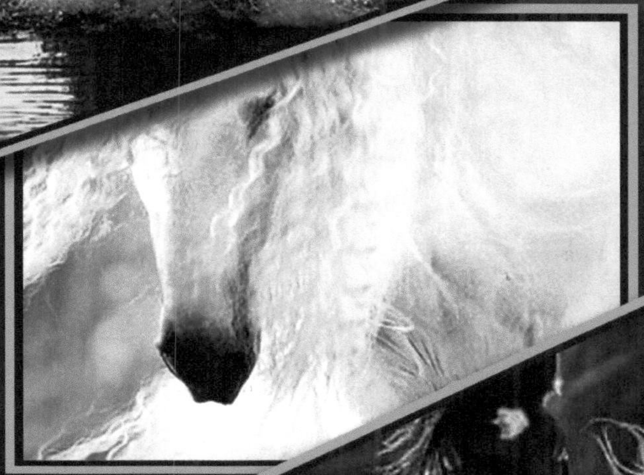

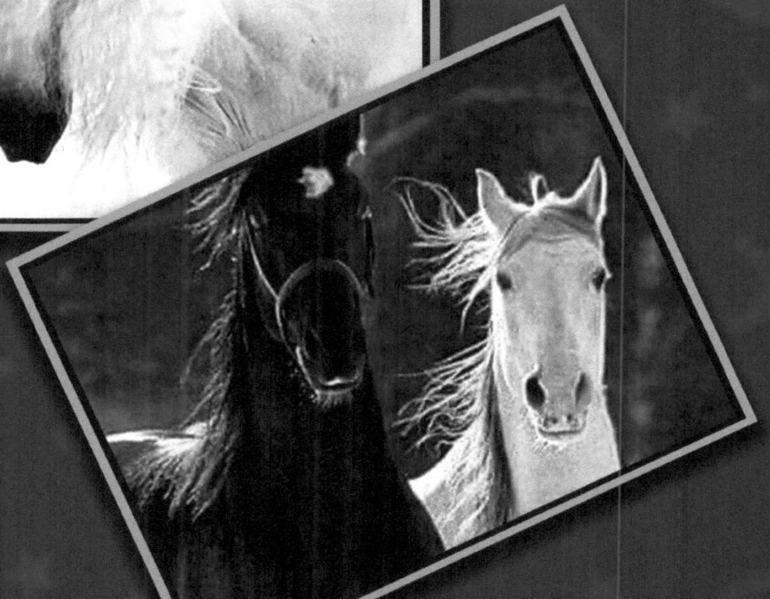

A GOOD HORSE IS THE BEST COMPANY IN THE WORLD.

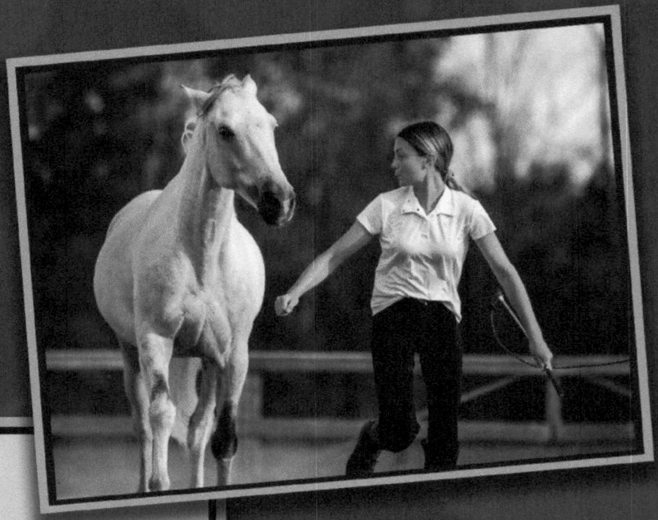

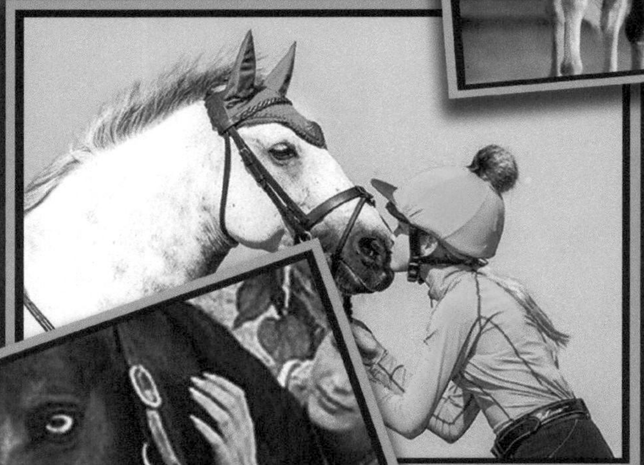

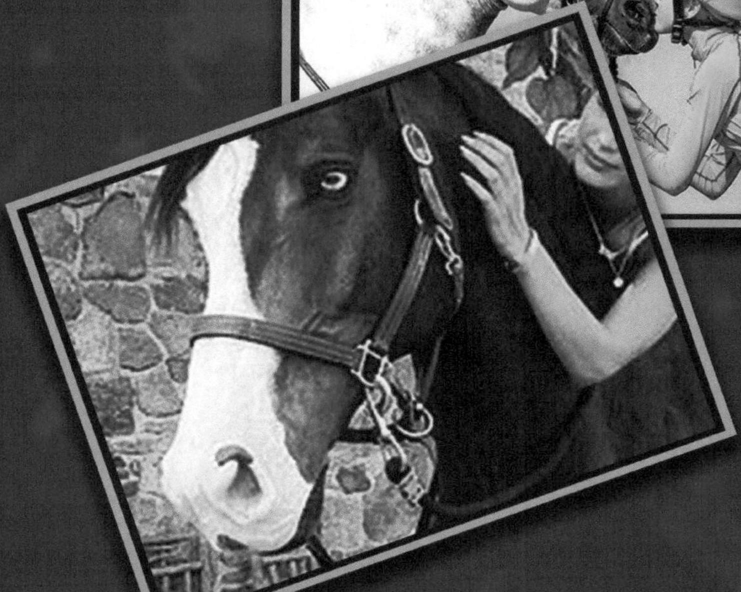

If you climb into the SADDLE

be ready for the RIDE.

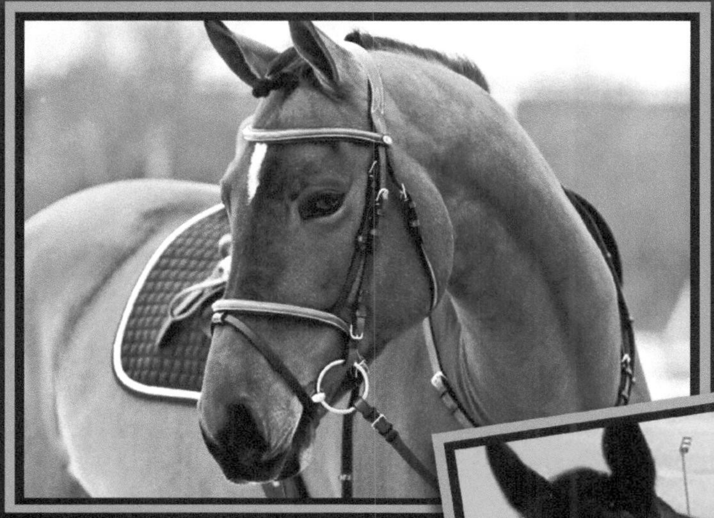

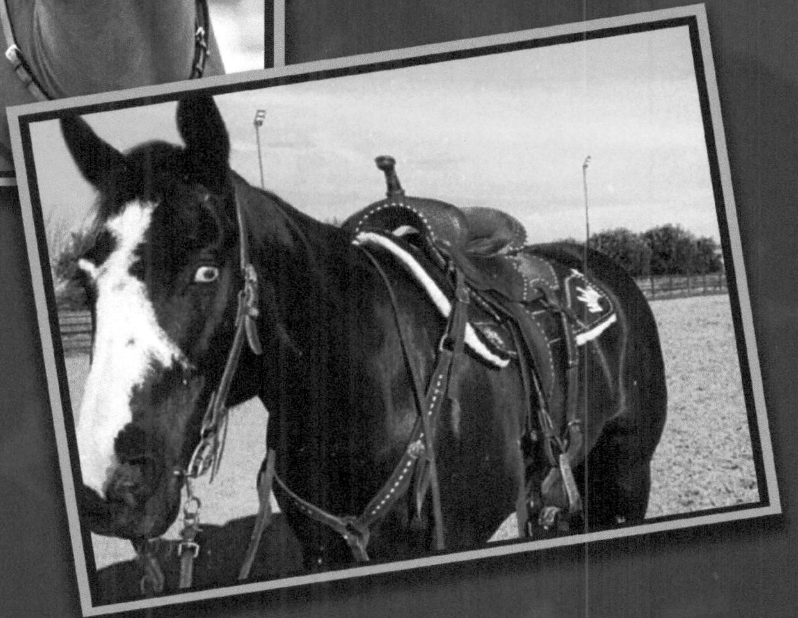

TRUE FRIENDS

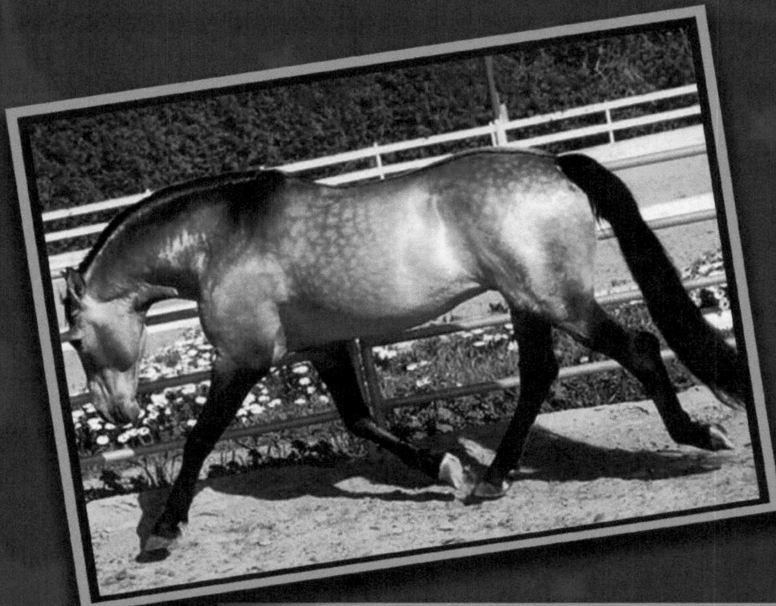

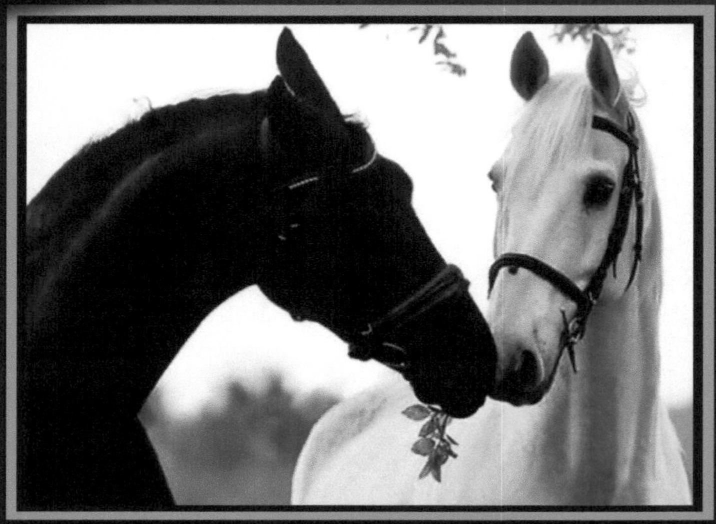

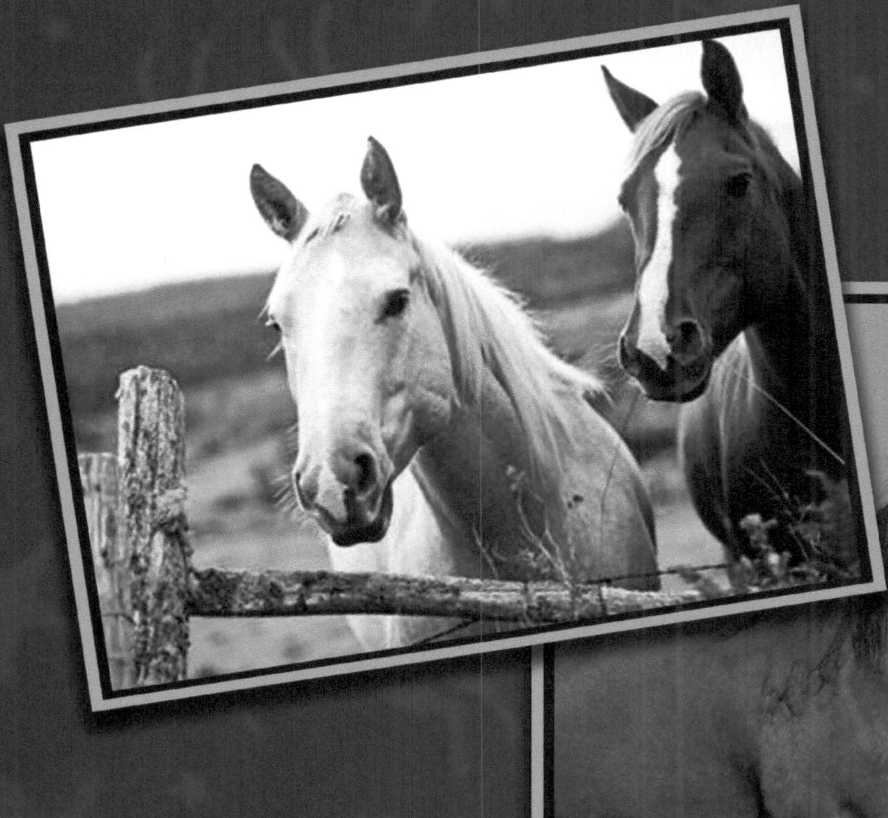

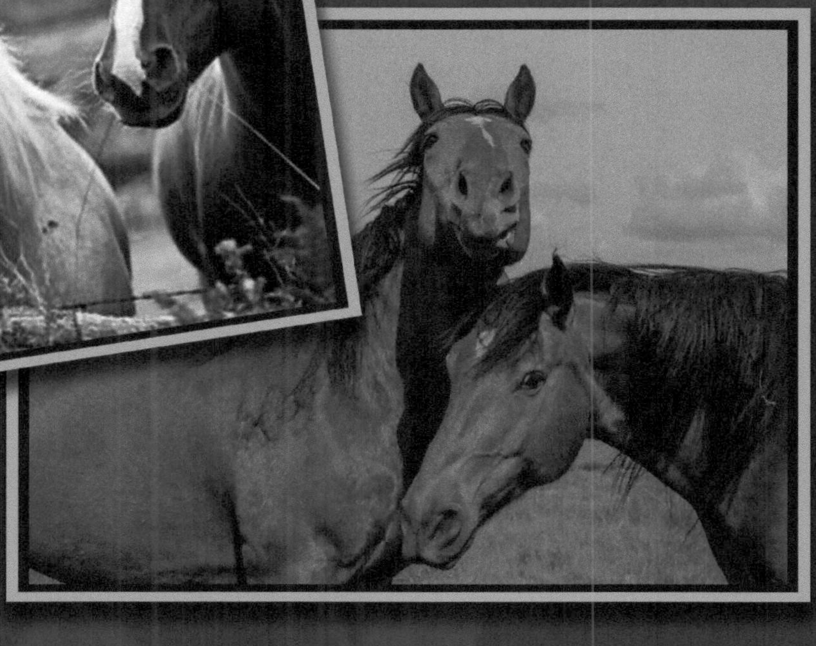

A good horse makes short miles.

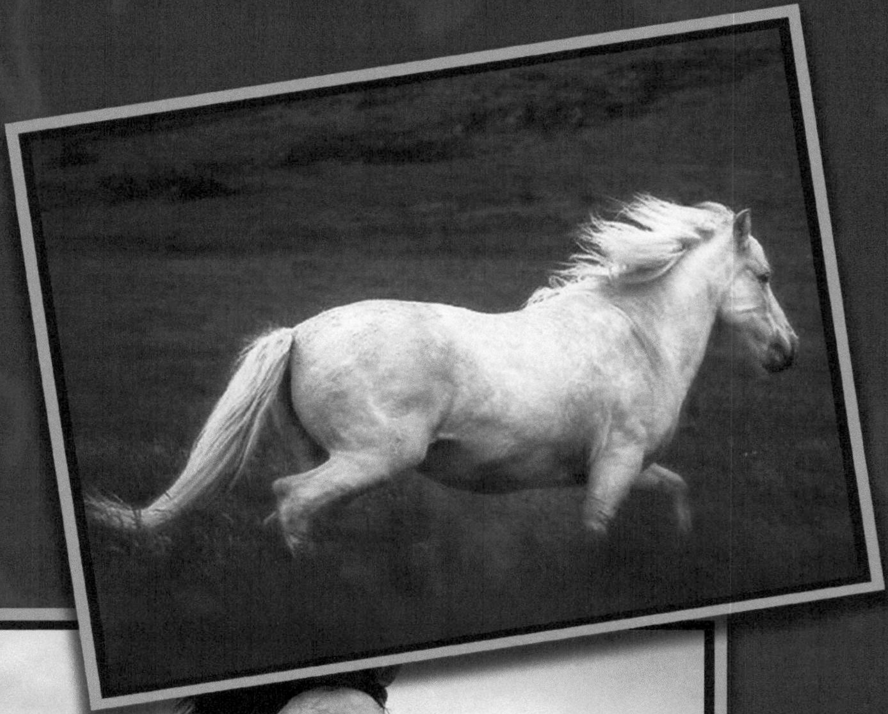

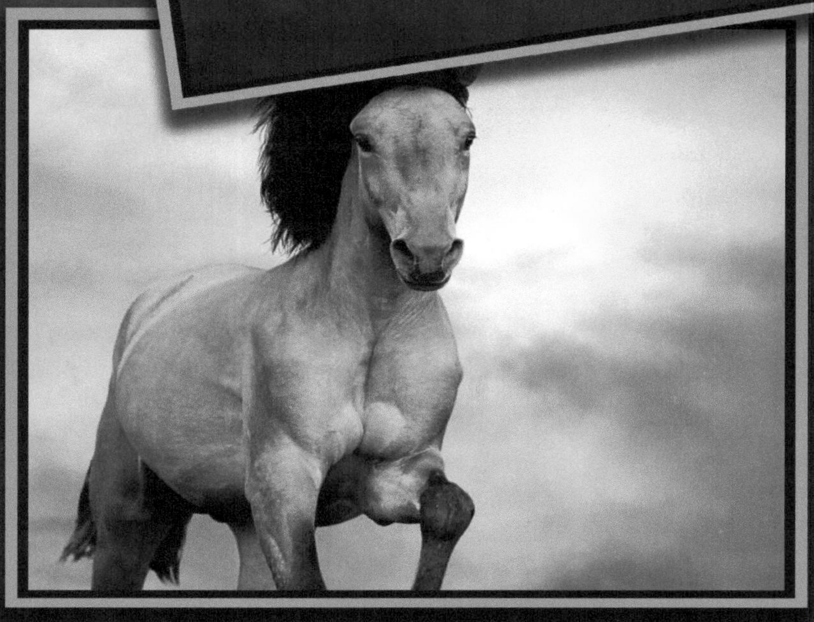

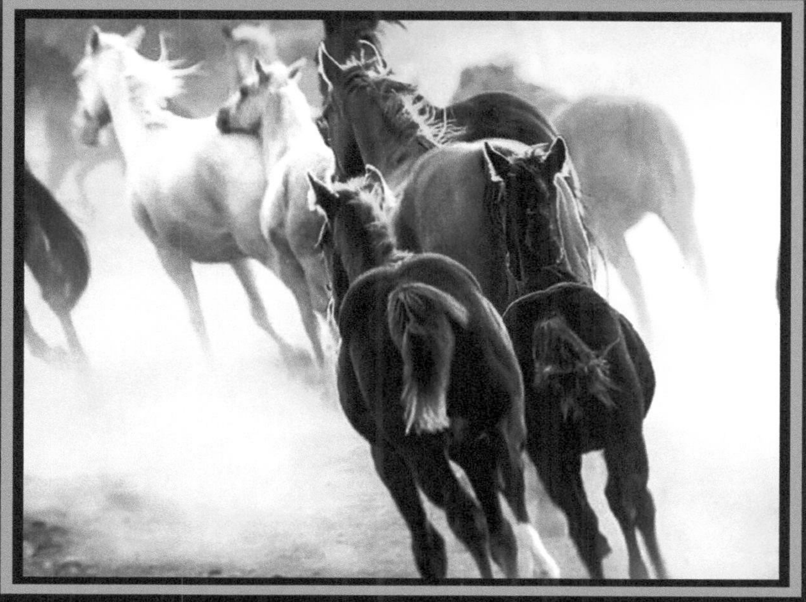

A horse never run so fast as when he has other horses to catch up and outplace.

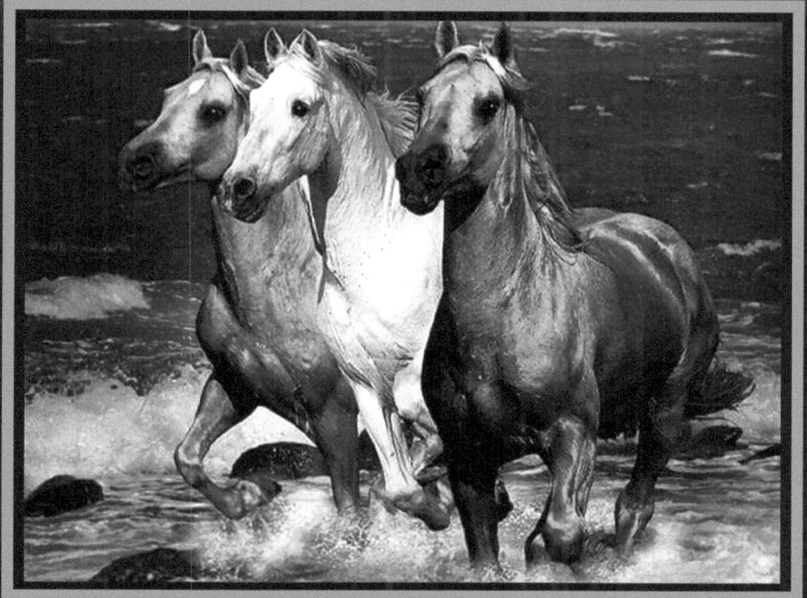

Give a horse what he needs and he will give you his heart in return.

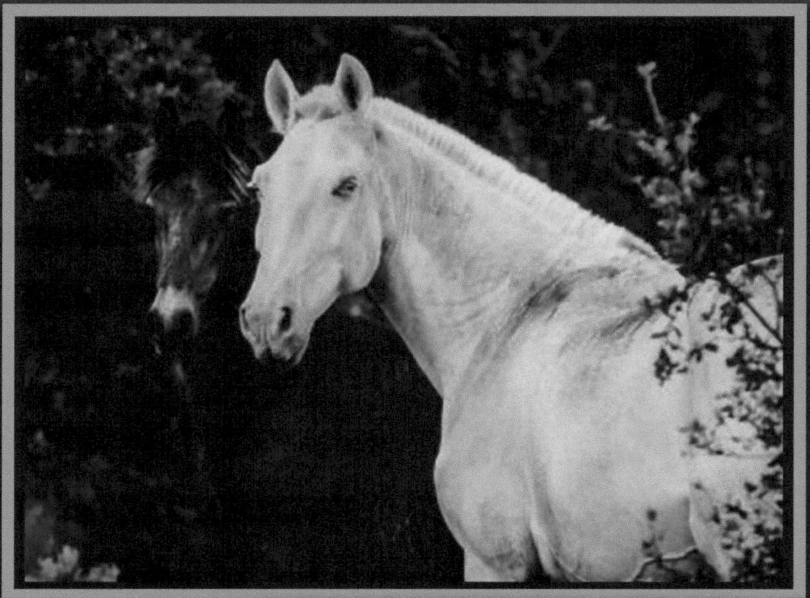

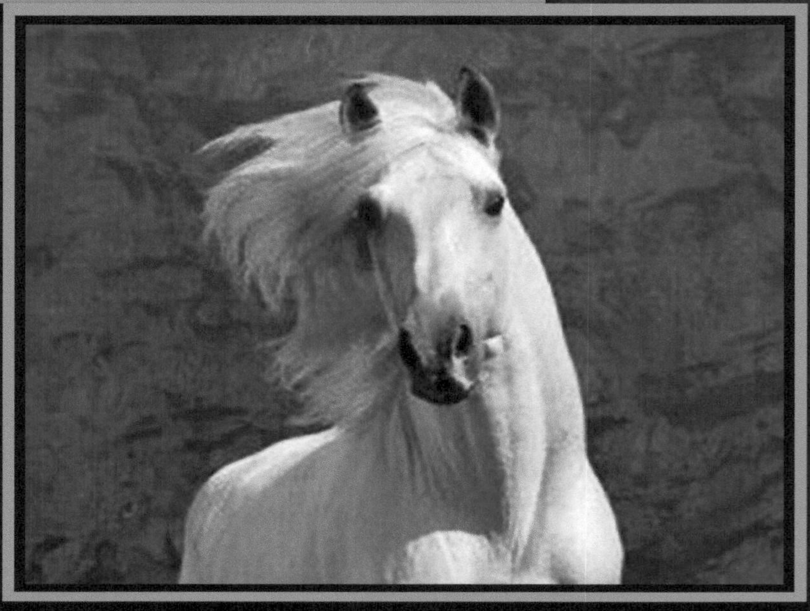

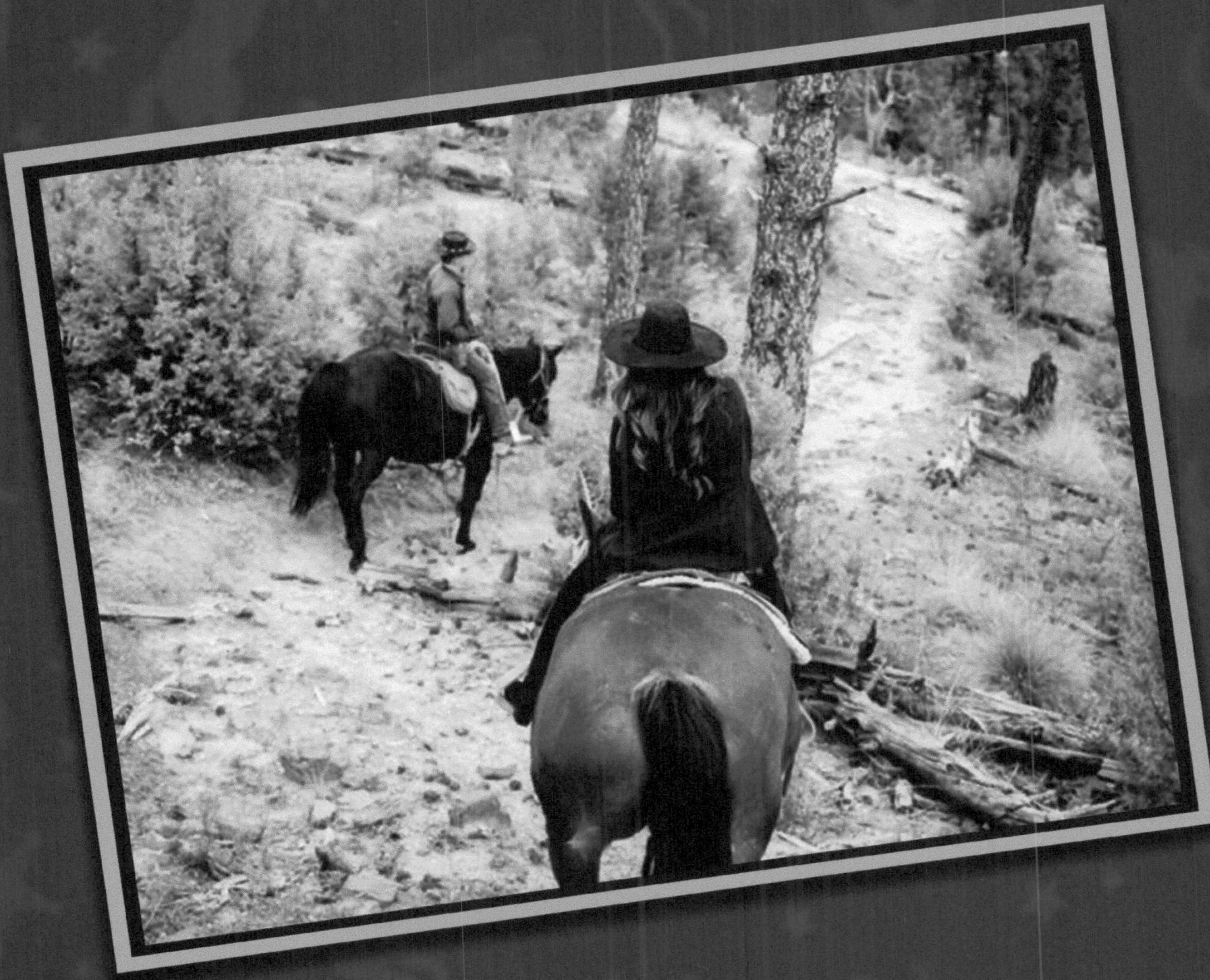

A right horse will build your confidence.

Run like a horse

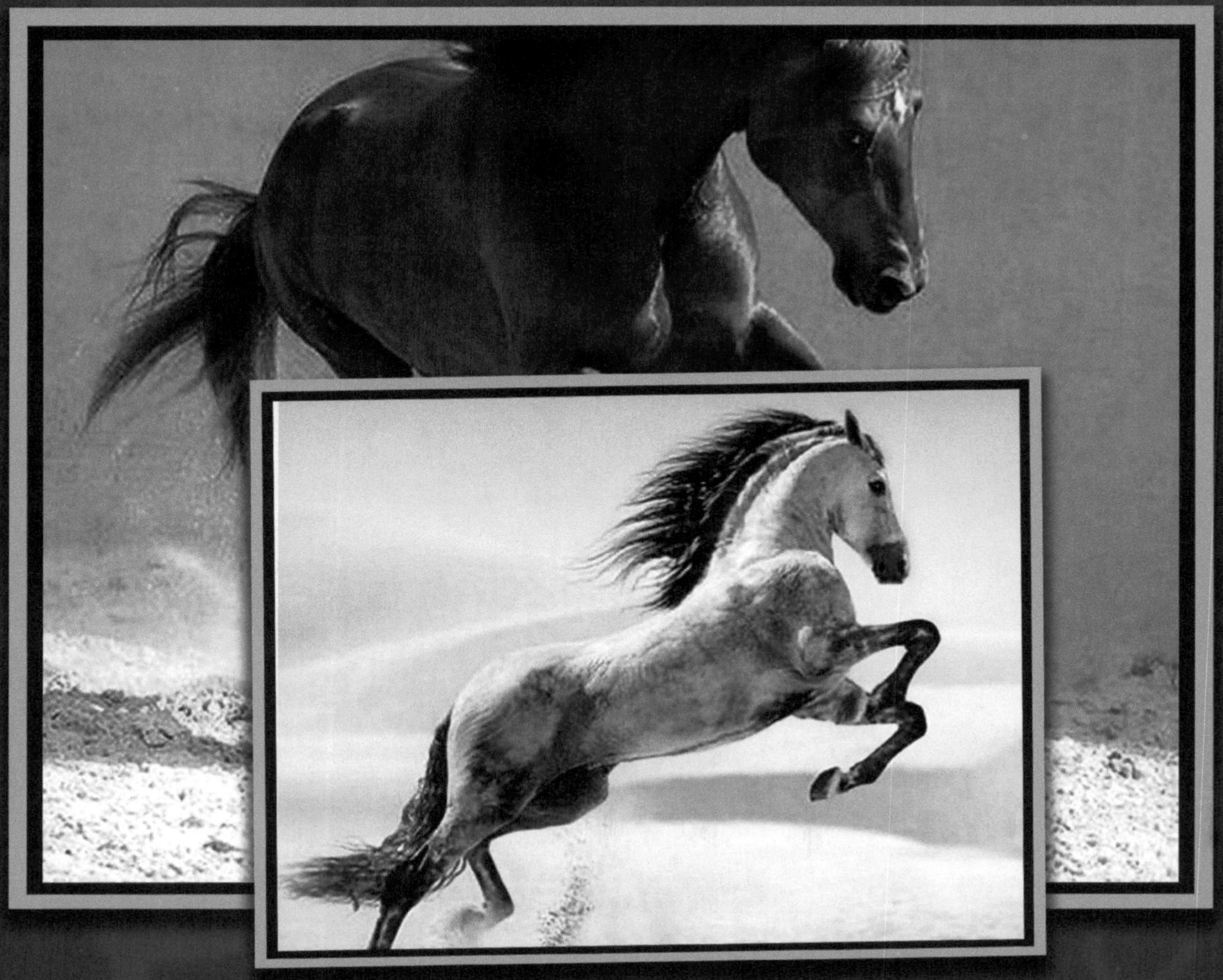

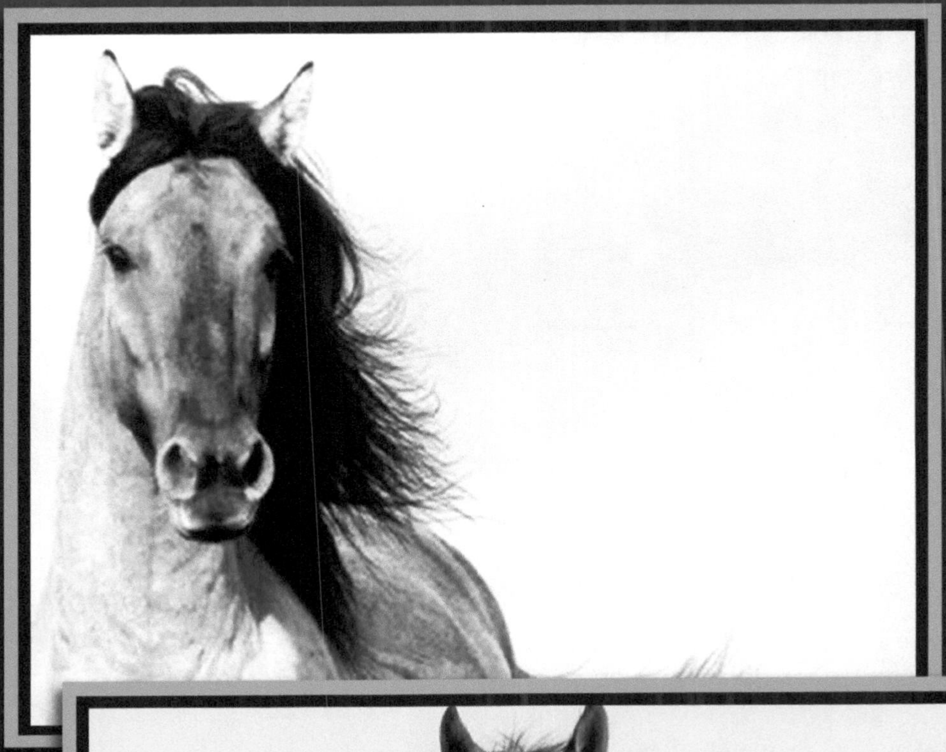

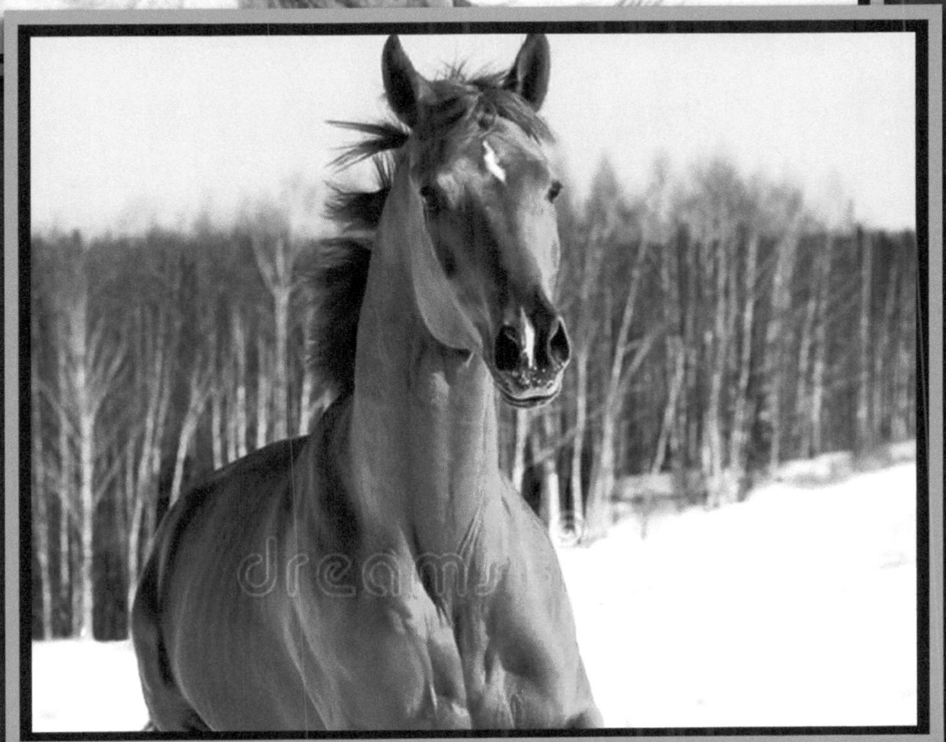

A dog may have men's best friend but the horse wrote history.

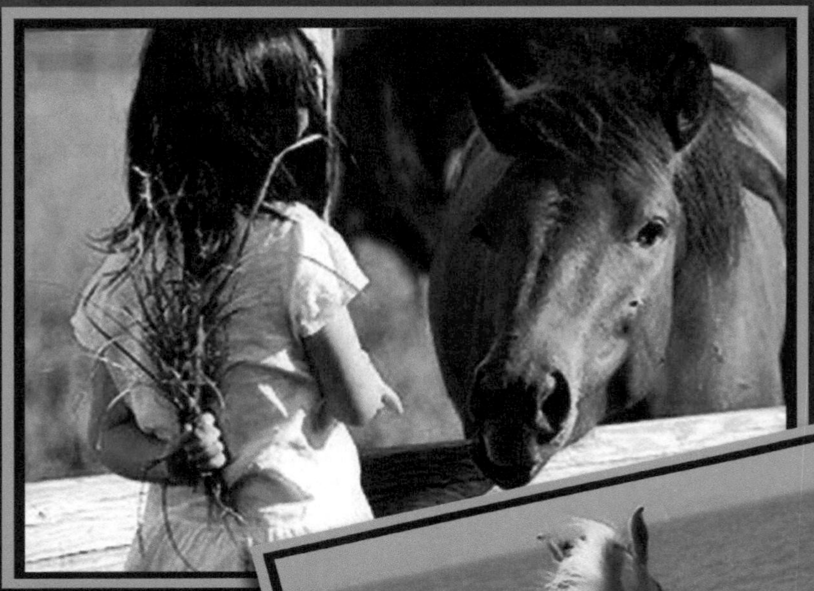

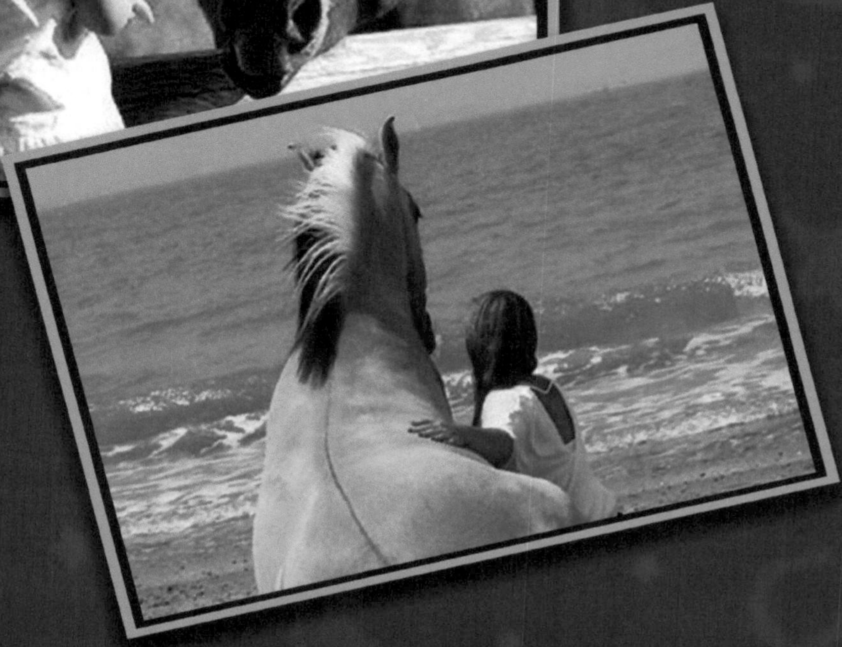

Nobody knows what true friendship is until they have been friend with a horse.

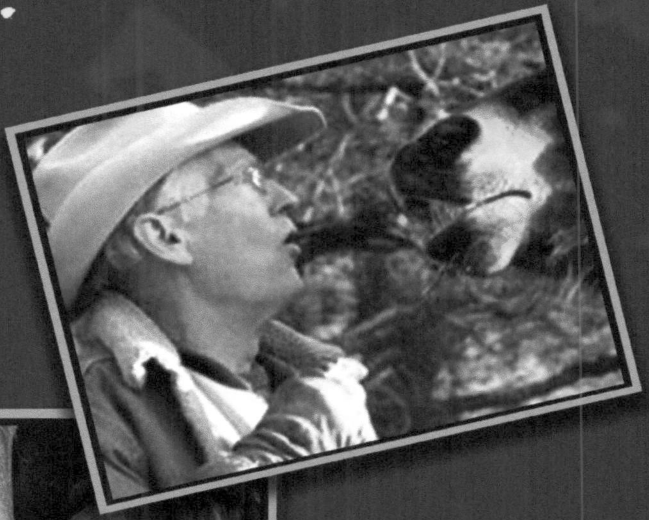

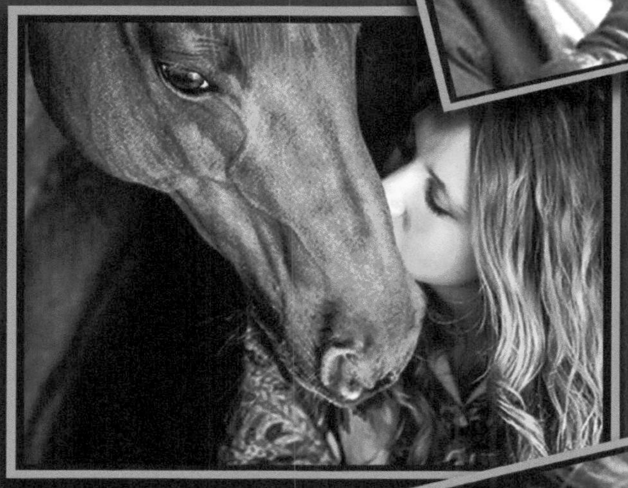

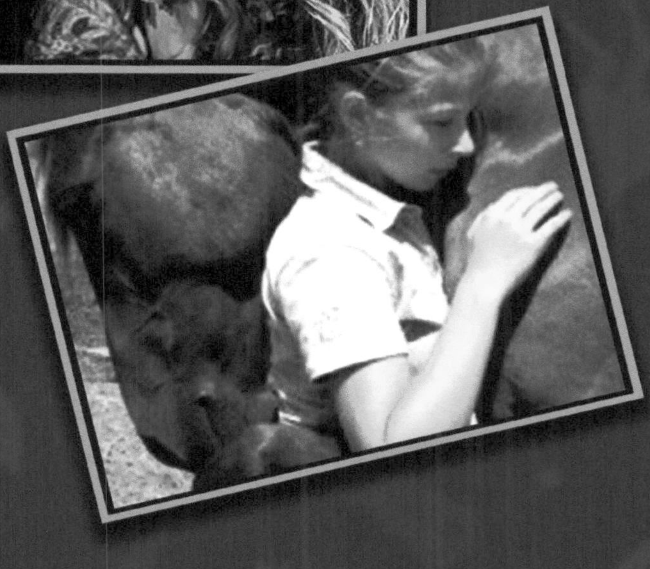

life is better with horse.

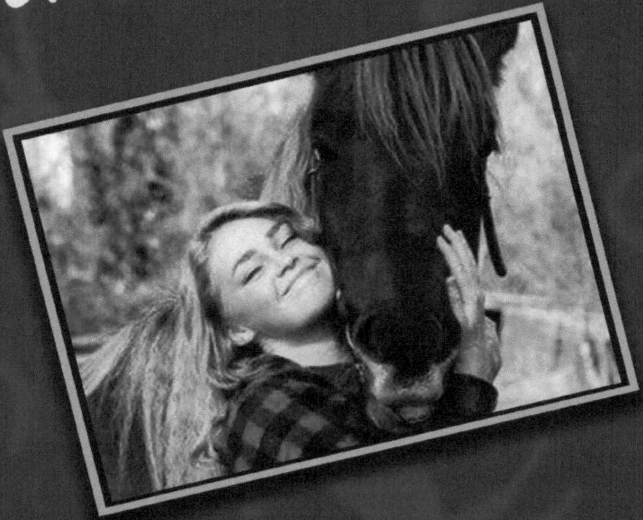

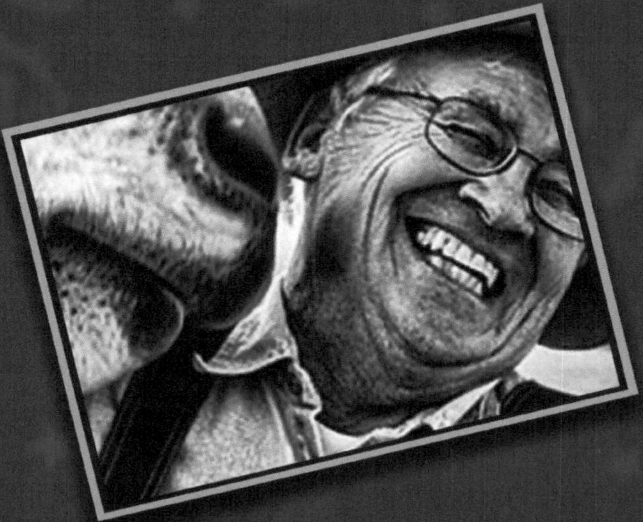

Horse make landscape look beautiful.

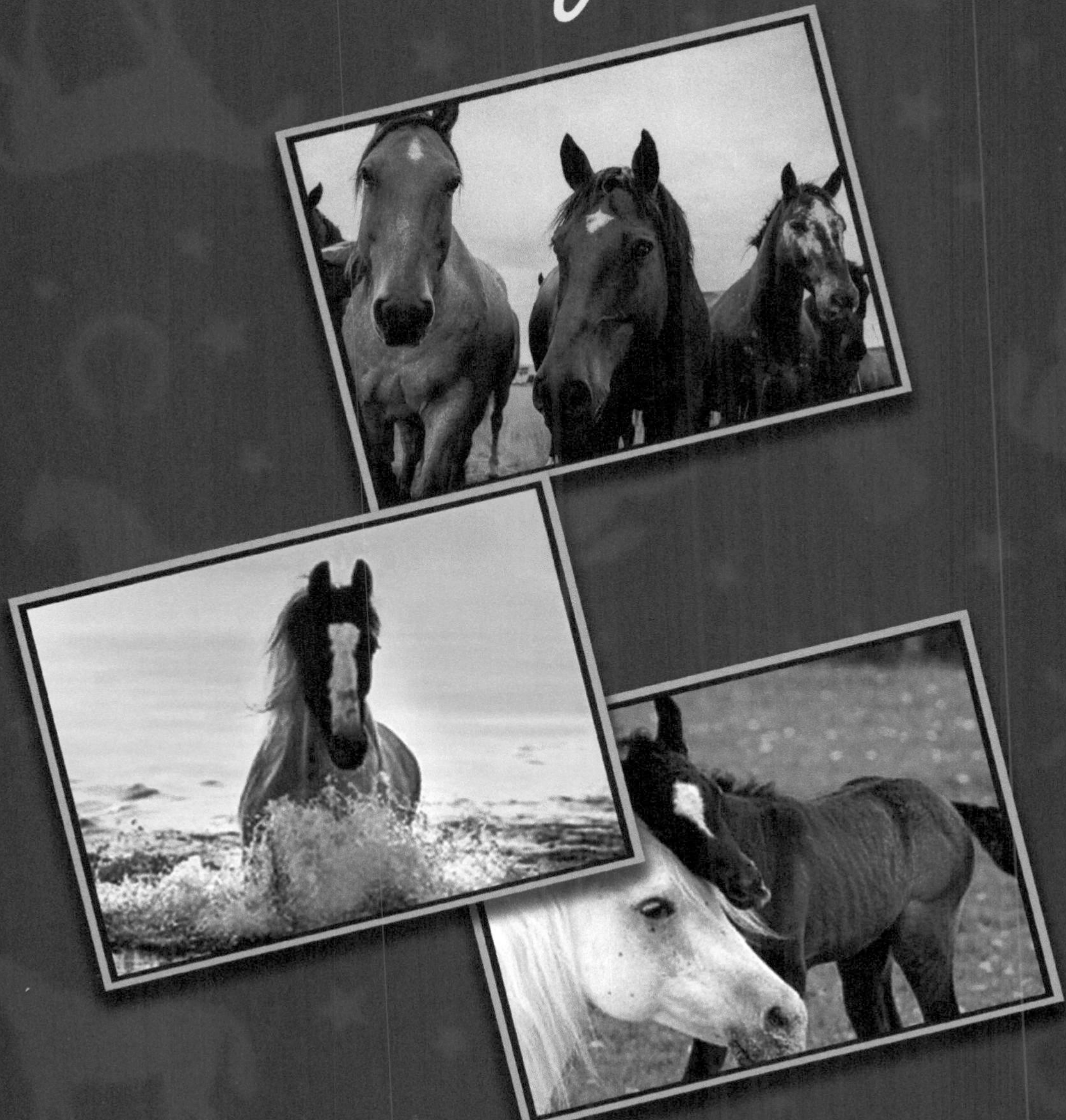

*If you have gained
the trust of a horse
you have friend for lide.*

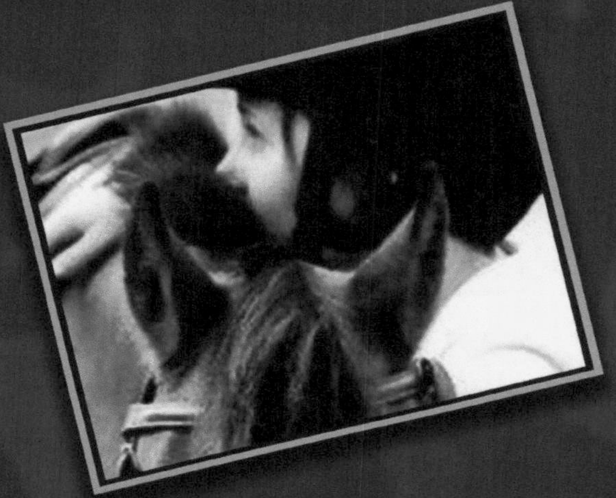

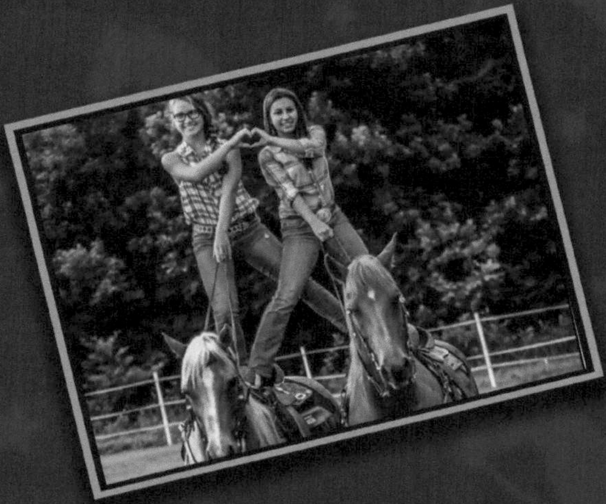

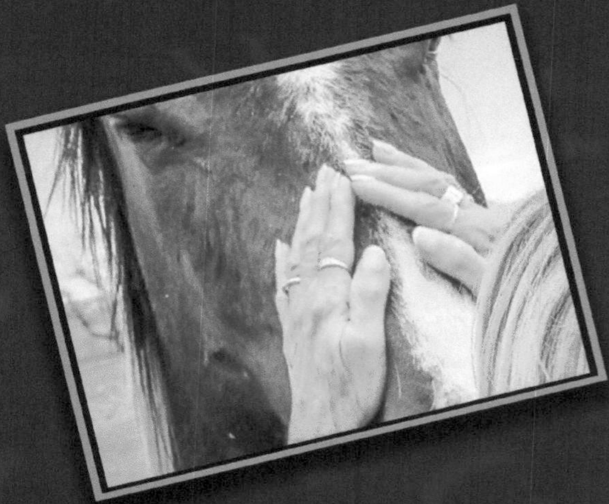

A horse is the projection of people dreams about themselves strong powerful beautiful

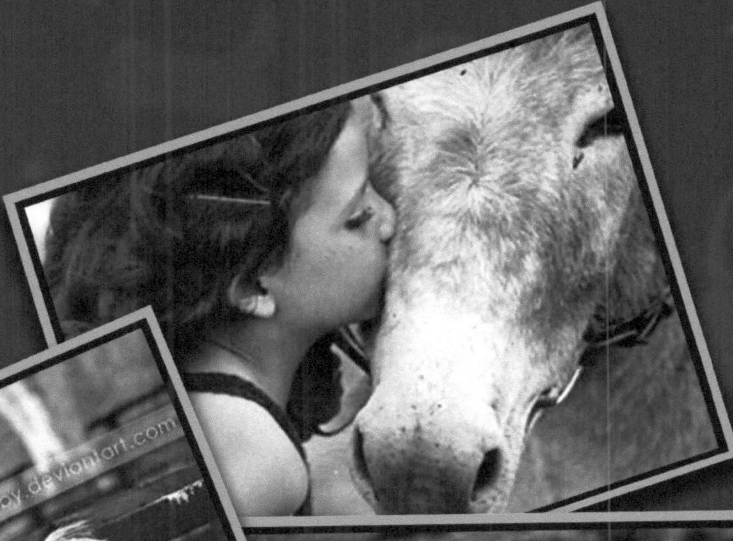

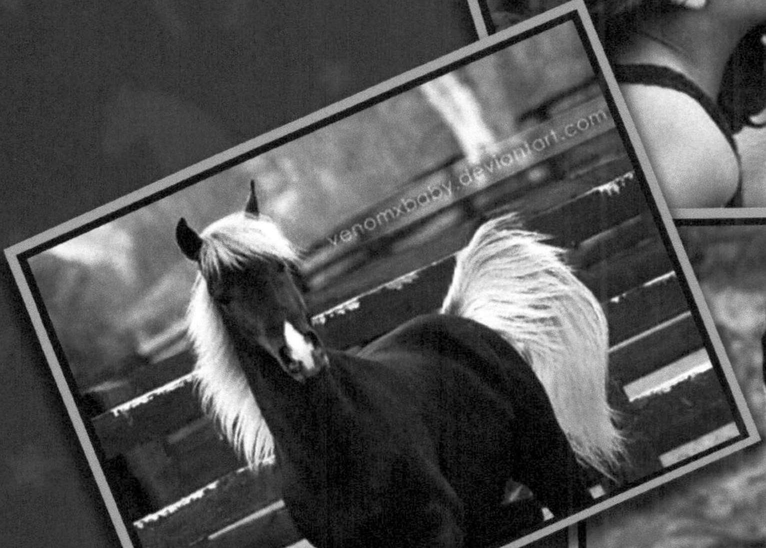

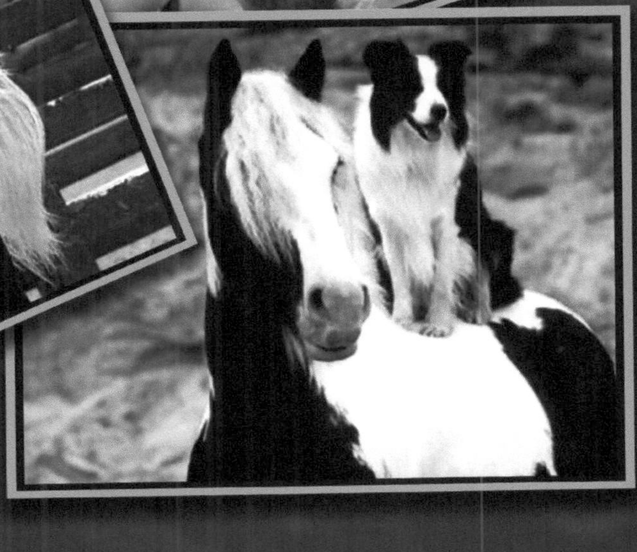

Horses fly without *wings*
and conquer without swords.

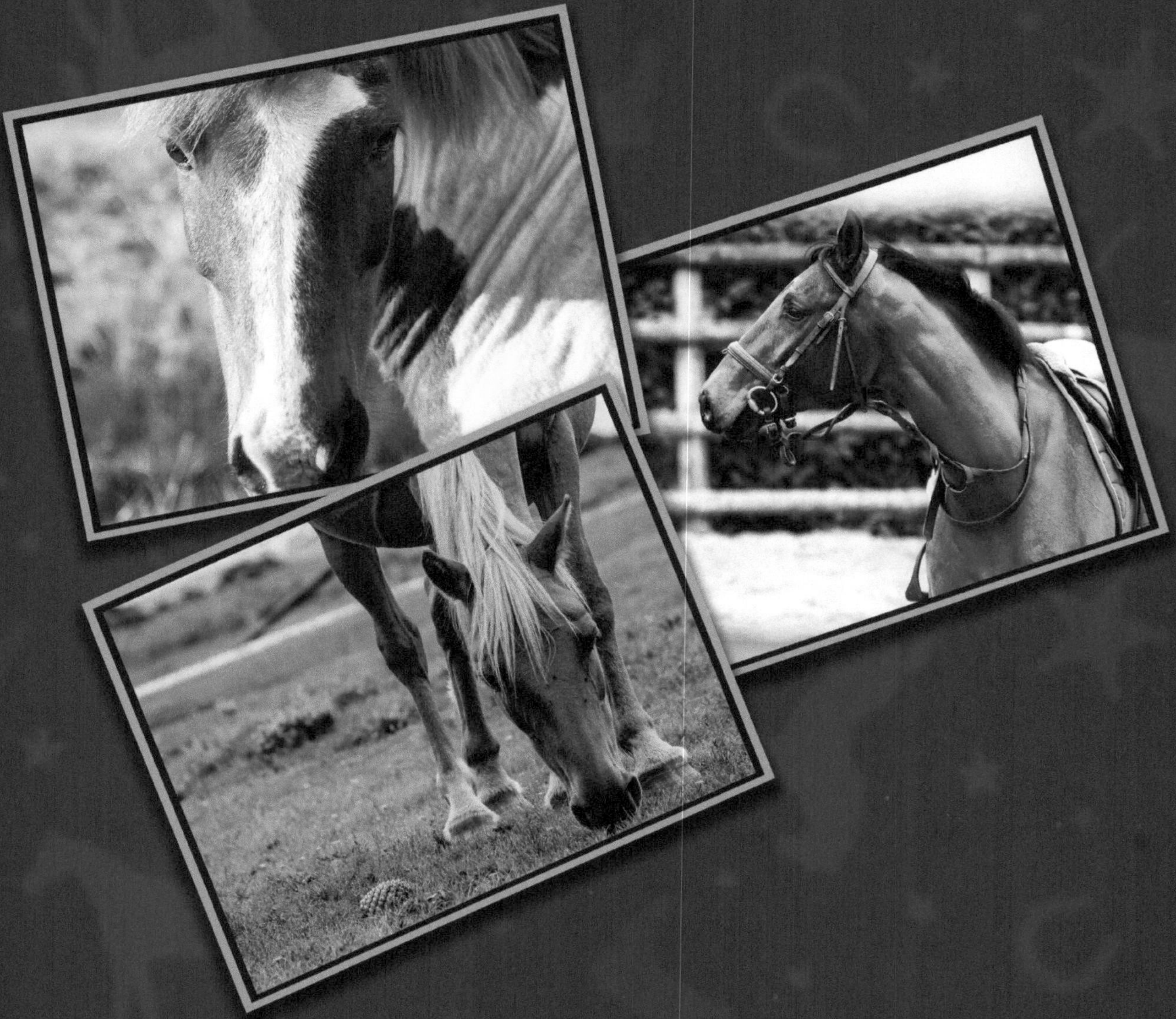

when you are on a great horse, you have the best seat you will ever have.

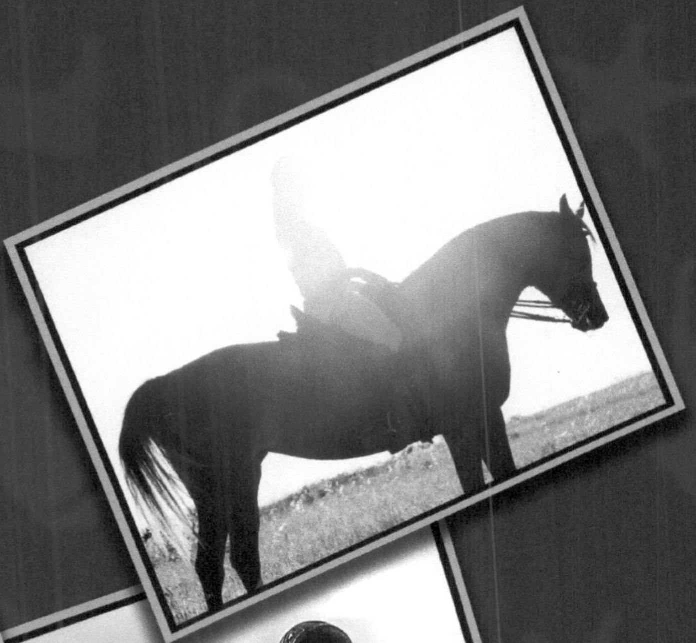
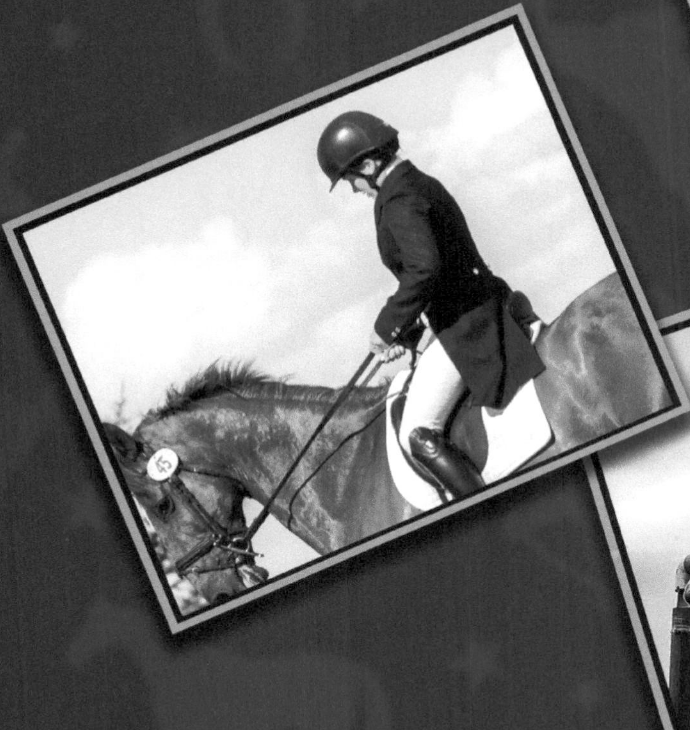
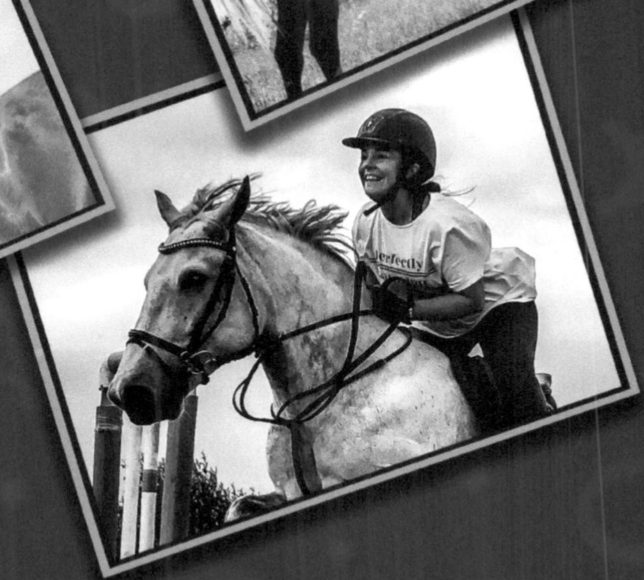

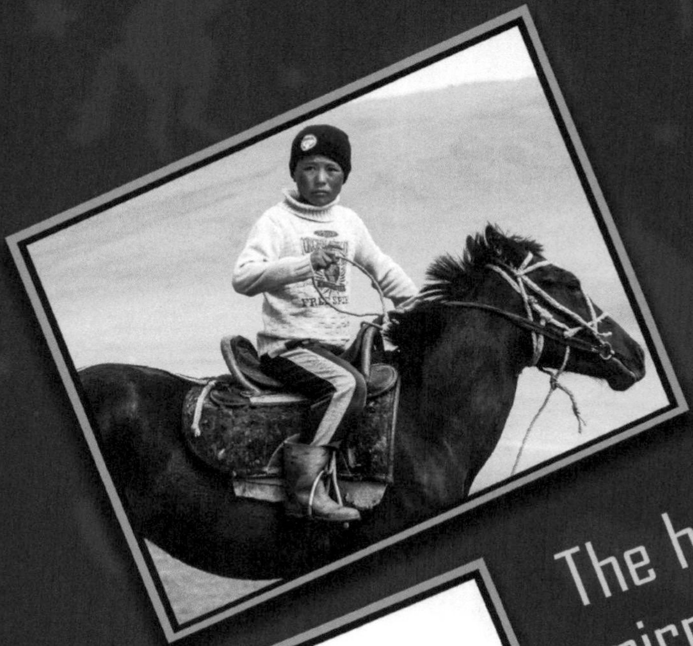

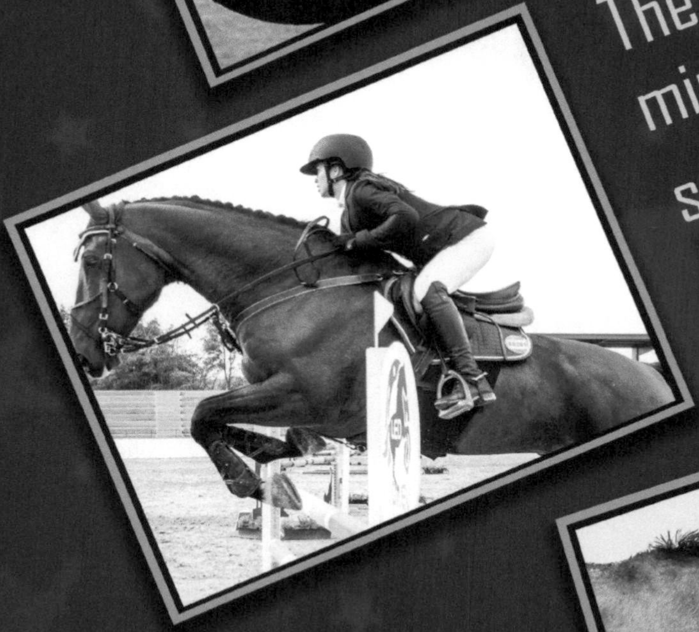

The horse is a
mirror to your
soul sometimes you might
not like what you see
sometimes you will.

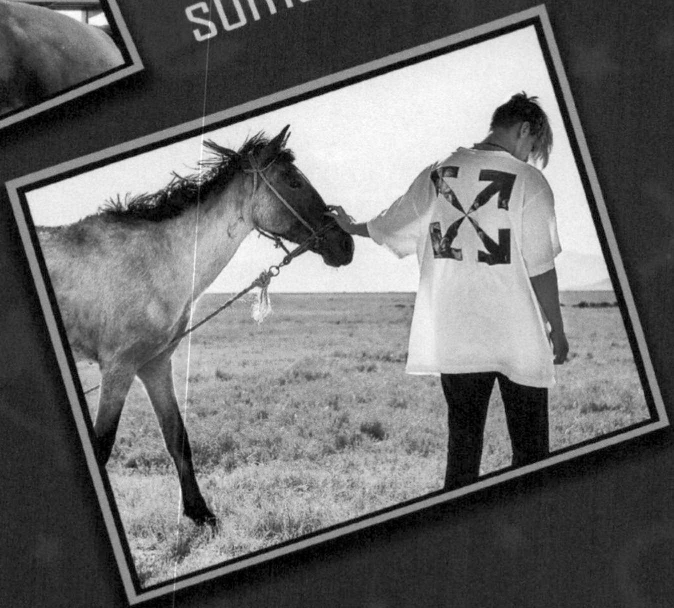

when you are on a great horse
you have the best seat you will
ever have.

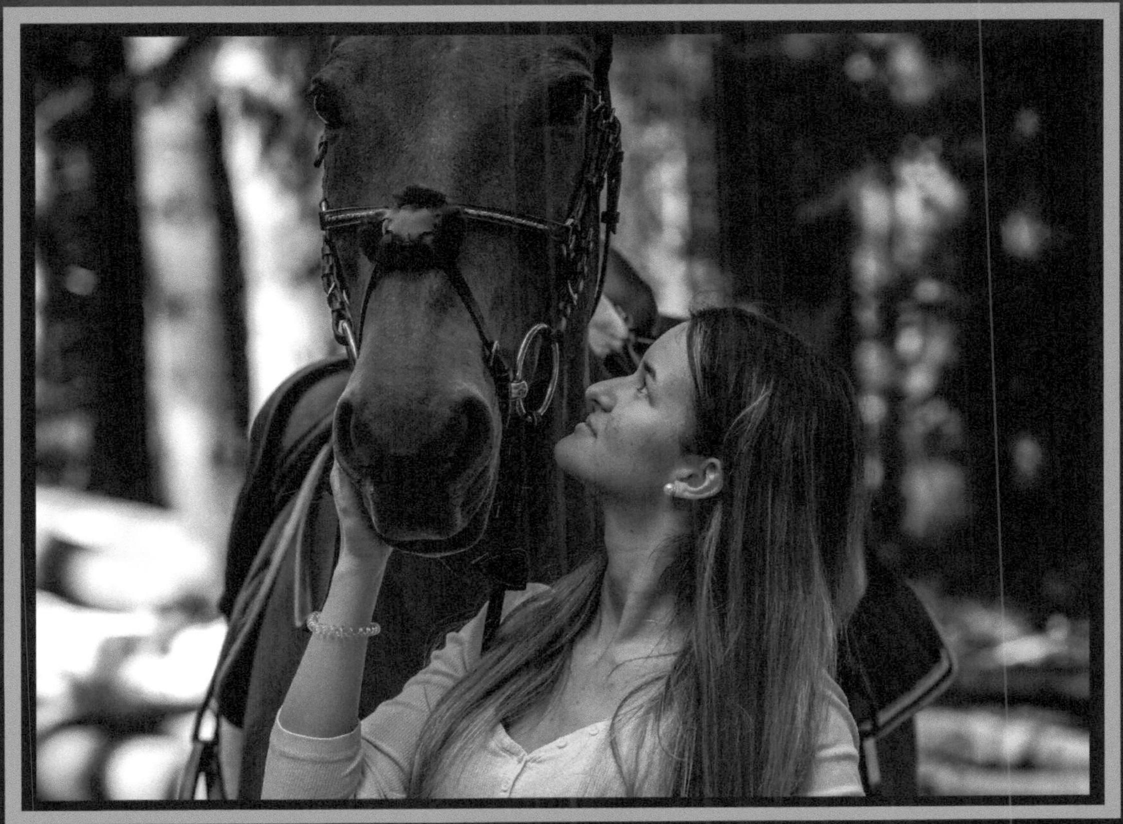

CPSIA information can be obtained
at www.ICGtesting.com
Printed in the USA
BVHW021120210621
610123BV00002B/87